TITLES

&

TREASURES

Painted Wings Publishing

FROM THE LIBRARY OF:

How to enjoy your literary treasures!

-The TBR Pile: 11 pages allow you to easily list 462 books 'To Be Read.'

-Challenges: Have fun completing 2 challenges for more variety in your book consumption!

-The Treasure Trove: Decorate with the top 50 books you read & journaled about.

-Journal Pages: 250 pages have been included to rate & review each book you read. Print off a picture of the cover & tape it in the designated spot, or lean on your artistic skills to recreate it!

-The Dusty DNFs (Did Not Finish): Not every book makes the cut for every reader. 6 pages are included (72 entries) for you to list the title and your progress before you decided to put the book down (e.g. 100/200 pages read, or 50%). A space is included for commentary.

-Extra Pages: 19 extra lined pages have been added in case those included for other topics didn't happen to be enough for your particular reading habits!

-Replacements & Recommendations: Other books & journals offered by the same publisher!

*For best results: use pens, pencils, or markers that are nonbleeding.

**For merch, extra tips, and free templates related to this book journal, go to JHouserWrites.com

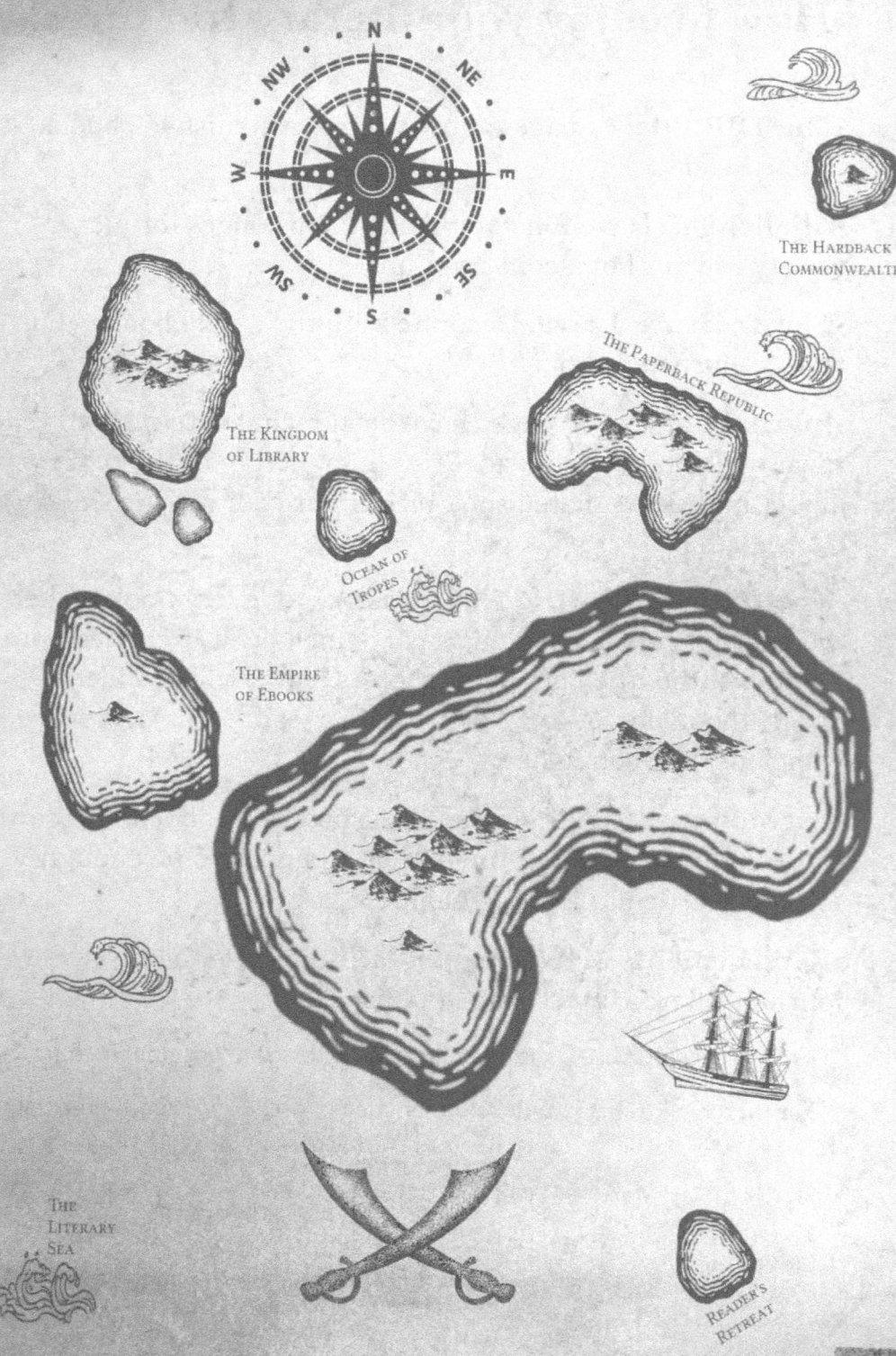

THE HARDBACK
COMMONWEALTH

THE PAPERBACK REPUBLIC

THE KINGDOM
OF LIBRARY

OCEAN OF
TROPES

THE EMPIRE
OF EBOOKS

THE
LITERARY
SEA

READER'S
RETREAT

 *** THE GREAT TBR LIST ***

 # * THE GREAT TBR LIST *

_____   _____

_____   _____

_____   _____

_____   _____

_____   _____

_____   _____

_____   _____

_____   _____

_____   _____

_____   _____

_____   _____

_____   _____

_____   _____

_____   _____

_____   _____

_____   _____

_____   _____

_____   _____

_____   _____

_____   _____

 # * THE GREAT TBR LIST *

 # * THE GREAT TBR LIST *

 # * THE GREAT TBR LIST *

 # * THE GREAT TBR LIST *

 # * THE GREAT TBR LIST *

_____   _____
_____   _____
_____   _____
_____   _____
_____   _____
_____   _____
_____   _____
_____   _____
_____   _____
_____   _____
_____   _____
_____   _____
_____   _____
_____   _____
_____   _____
_____   _____
_____   _____
_____   _____
_____   _____
_____   _____
_____   _____

 # * THE GREAT TBR LIST *

_____   _____
_____   _____
_____   _____
_____   _____
_____   _____
_____   _____
_____   _____
_____   _____
_____   _____
_____   _____
_____   _____
_____   _____
_____   _____
_____   _____
_____   _____
_____   _____
_____   _____
_____   _____

 # * THE GREAT TBR LIST *

 # * THE GREAT TBR LIST *

 # * THE GREAT TBR LIST *

_____   _____

_____   _____

_____   _____

_____   _____

_____   _____

_____   _____

_____   _____

_____   _____

_____   _____

_____   _____

_____   _____

_____   _____

_____   _____

_____   _____

_____   _____

_____   _____

_____   _____

_____   _____

_____   _____

THE RAINBOW CHALLENGE

Read a book with a cover featuring every color of the rainbow!

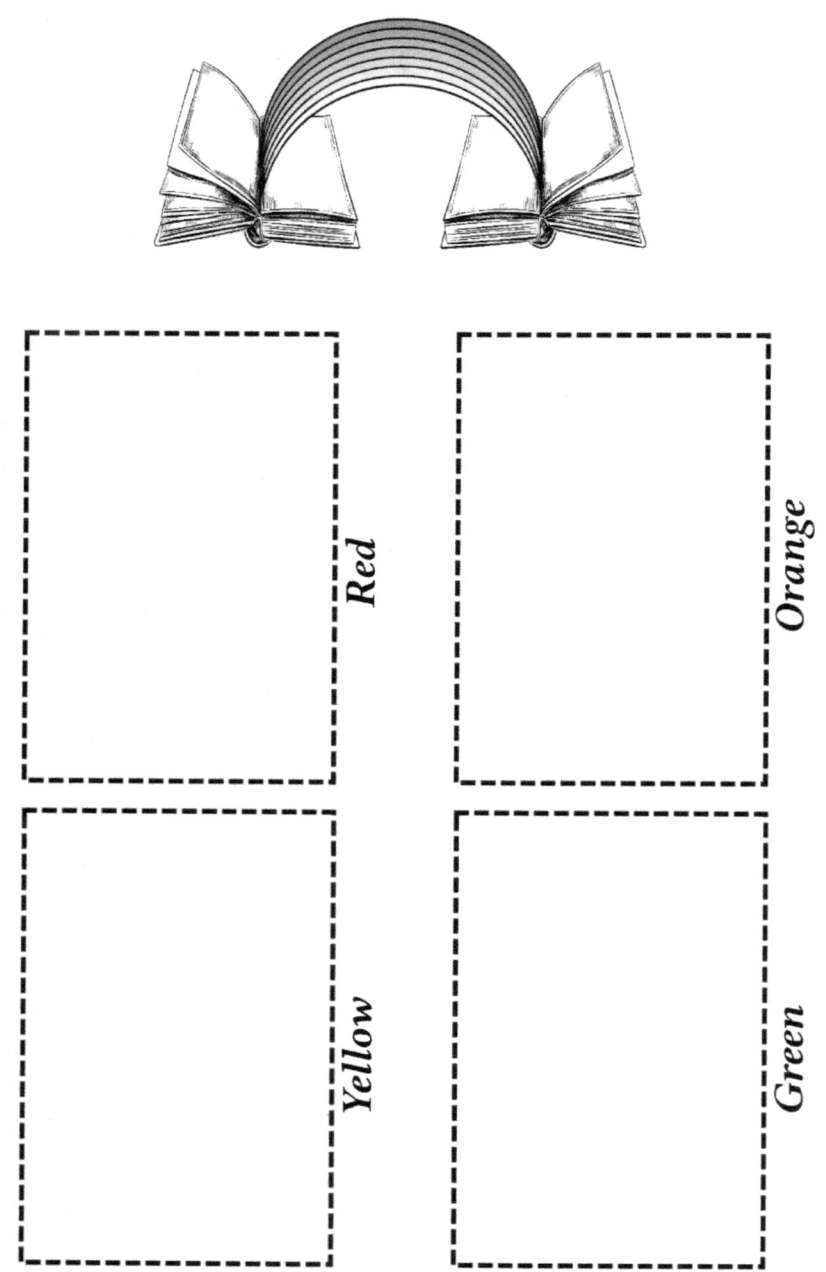

Red

Orange

Yellow

Green

Blue

Violet

Black

Indigo

White

Multicolor

THE ALPHABET CHALLENGE

Read a book with a title starting with each letter of the alphabet!

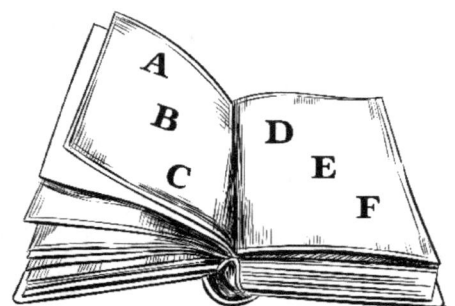

A _____   N _____

B _____   O _____

C _____   P _____

D _____   Q _____

E _____   R _____

F _____   S _____

G _____   T _____

H _____   U _____

I _____   V _____

J _____   W _____

K _____   X _____

L _____   Y _____

M _____   Z _____

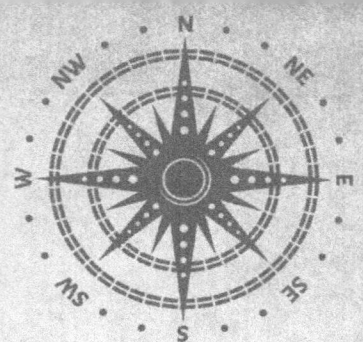

The Paperback Republic

ENJOY

Ocean of
Tropes

THE

ADVENTURE!

Fiction Island

TITLE: _____

GENRE: _____

SERIES: _____

AUTHOR: _____

PAGES: _____

STARTED: _____

FINISHED: _____

☆☆☆☆☆

FORMAT READ: EBOOK / PRINT / AUDIOBOOK

✔ SYNOPSIS/THINGS I LIKED: _____

_____

_____

_____

🚫 THINGS I DIDN'T LIKE: _____

_____

_____

_____

✎ FAVORITE QUOTE(S): _____

_____

_____

_____

_____

_____

_____

_____

TITLE: _____

GENRE: _____

SERIES: _____

AUTHOR: _____

PAGES: _____

STARTED: _____

FINISHED: _____

☆ ☆ ☆ ☆ ☆

FORMAT READ: EBOOK / PRINT / AUDIOBOOK

✓ **SYNOPSIS/THINGS I LIKED:** _____

_____

_____

_____

_____

🚫 **THINGS I DIDN'T LIKE:** _____

_____

_____

_____

_____

📝 **FAVORITE QUOTE(S):** _____

_____

_____

_____

_____

_____

_____

_____

_____

✓ **Synopsis/Things I liked:**

_____
_____
_____
_____
_____

🚫 **Things I didn't like:**

_____
_____
_____
_____
_____

✏️ **Favorite quote(s):**

_____
_____
_____
_____
_____
_____
_____
_____

Title: _____

Genre: _____

Series: _____

Author: _____

Pages: _____

Started: _____

Finished: _____

☆☆☆☆☆

☑ **Synopsis/Things I liked:**

_____
_____
_____
_____

🚫 **Things I didn't like:**

_____
_____
_____
_____

✎ **Favorite quote(s):**

_____
_____
_____
_____
_____
_____

Title: _____

Genre: _____

Series: _____

Author: _____

Pages: _____

Started: _____

Finished: _____

☆ ☆ ☆ ☆ ☆

Format read: Ebook / Print / Audiobook

4

TITLE: _____

GENRE: _____

SERIES: _____

AUTHOR: _____

PAGES: _____

STARTED: _____

FINISHED: _____

☆ ☆ ☆ ☆ ☆

FORMAT READ: EBOOK / PRINT / AUDIOBOOK

✔ **SYNOPSIS/THINGS I LIKED:**

_____

_____

_____

_____

_____

🚫 **THINGS I DIDN'T LIKE:**

_____

_____

_____

_____

_____

✎ **FAVORITE QUOTE(S):**

_____

_____

_____

_____

_____

_____

_____

_____

TITLE: _____

GENRE: _____

SERIES: _____

AUTHOR: _____

PAGES: _____

STARTED: _____

FINISHED: _____

☆☆☆☆☆

FORMAT READ: EBOOK / PRINT / AUDIOBOOK

✓ **SYNOPSIS/THINGS I LIKED:**

_____
_____
_____
_____

🚫 **THINGS I DIDN'T LIKE:**

_____
_____
_____
_____

✏️ **FAVORITE QUOTE(S):**

_____
_____
_____
_____
_____
_____

✔ **SYNOPSIS/THINGS I LIKED:**

_____
_____
_____
_____
_____

🚫 **THINGS I DIDN'T LIKE:**

_____
_____
_____
_____

📝 **FAVORITE QUOTE(S):**

_____
_____
_____
_____
_____
_____
_____

TITLE: _____

GENRE: _____

SERIES: _____

AUTHOR: _____

PAGES: _____

STARTED: _____

FINISHED: _____

☆ ☆ ☆ ☆ ☆

FORMAT READ: EBOOK / PRINT / AUDIOBOOK 7

✅ **SYNOPSIS/THINGS I LIKED:**

_____

_____

_____

_____

_____

🚫 **THINGS I DIDN'T LIKE:**

_____

_____

_____

_____

✏️ **FAVORITE QUOTE(S):**

_____

_____

_____

_____

_____

_____

_____

TITLE: _____

GENRE: _____

SERIES: _____

AUTHOR: _____

PAGES: _____

STARTED: _____

FINISHED: _____

☆ ☆ ☆ ☆ ☆

FORMAT READ: EBOOK / PRINT / AUDIOBOOK

TITLE: _____

GENRE: _____

SERIES: _____

AUTHOR: _____

PAGES: _____

STARTED: _____

FINISHED: _____

☆ ☆ ☆ ☆ ☆

FORMAT READ: EBOOK / PRINT / AUDIOBOOK

✓ SYNOPSIS/THINGS I LIKED: _____

_____

_____

_____

_____

🚫 THINGS I DIDN'T LIKE: _____

_____

_____

_____

_____

✏️ FAVORITE QUOTE(S): _____

_____

_____

_____

_____

_____

_____

_____

TITLE: _____

GENRE: _____

SERIES: _____

AUTHOR: _____

PAGES: _____

STARTED: _____

FINISHED: _____

☆ ☆ ☆ ☆ ☆

FORMAT READ: EBOOK / PRINT / AUDIOBOOK

✔ **SYNOPSIS/THINGS I LIKED:**

_____
_____
_____
_____

🚫 **THINGS I DIDN'T LIKE:**

_____
_____
_____
_____

📝 **FAVORITE QUOTE(S):**

_____
_____
_____
_____
_____
_____
_____
_____

☑ **SYNOPSIS/THINGS I LIKED:**

_____
_____
_____
_____
_____

🚫 **THINGS I DIDN'T LIKE:**

_____
_____
_____
_____

✏️ **FAVORITE QUOTE(S):**

_____
_____
_____
_____
_____
_____

TITLE: _____

GENRE: _____

SERIES: _____

AUTHOR: _____

PAGES: _____

STARTED: _____

FINISHED: _____

☆ ☆ ☆ ☆ ☆

✅ **SYNOPSIS/THINGS I LIKED:**

_____
_____
_____
_____
_____

🚫 **THINGS I DIDN'T LIKE:**

_____
_____
_____
_____
_____

📝 **FAVORITE QUOTE(S):**

_____
_____
_____
_____
_____
_____
_____
_____

TITLE: _____

GENRE: _____

SERIES: _____

AUTHOR: _____

PAGES: _____

STARTED: _____

FINISHED: _____

☆ ☆ ☆ ☆ ☆

FORMAT READ: EBOOK / PRINT / AUDIOBOOK

TITLE: _____

GENRE: _____

SERIES: _____

AUTHOR: _____

PAGES: _____

STARTED: _____

FINISHED: _____

☆☆☆☆☆

FORMAT READ: EBOOK / PRINT / AUDIOBOOK

✓ SYNOPSIS/THINGS I LIKED: _____

_____

_____

_____

_____

🚫 THINGS I DIDN'T LIKE: _____

_____

_____

_____

_____

✏️ FAVORITE QUOTE(S): _____

_____

_____

_____

_____

_____

_____

_____

TITLE: _____

GENRE: _____

SERIES: _____

AUTHOR: _____

PAGES: _____

STARTED: _____

FINISHED: _____

☆ ☆ ☆ ☆ ☆

FORMAT READ: EBOOK / PRINT / AUDIOBOOK

✔ SYNOPSIS/THINGS I LIKED:

_____
_____
_____
_____
_____

🚫 THINGS I DIDN'T LIKE:

_____
_____
_____
_____

✎ FAVORITE QUOTE(S):

_____
_____
_____
_____
_____
_____
_____

☑ **SYNOPSIS/THINGS I LIKED:**

_____
_____
_____
_____
_____

🚫 **THINGS I DIDN'T LIKE:**

_____
_____
_____
_____

✏️ **FAVORITE QUOTE(S):**

_____
_____
_____
_____
_____
_____
_____
_____

TITLE: _____

GENRE: _____

SERIES: _____

AUTHOR: _____

PAGES: _____

STARTED: _____

FINISHED: _____

☆ ☆ ☆ ☆ ☆

FORMAT READ: EBOOK / PRINT / AUDIOBOOK **15**

✔ **SYNOPSIS/THINGS I LIKED:**

_____

_____

_____

_____

_____

🚫 **THINGS I DIDN'T LIKE:**

_____

_____

_____

_____

📝 **FAVORITE QUOTE(S):**

_____

_____

_____

_____

_____

_____

_____

TITLE: _____

GENRE: _____

SERIES: _____

AUTHOR: _____

PAGES: _____

STARTED: _____

FINISHED: _____

☆ ☆ ☆ ☆ ☆

FORMAT READ: EBOOK / PRINT / AUDIOBOOK

TITLE: _____

GENRE: _____

SERIES: _____

AUTHOR: _____

PAGES: _____

STARTED: _____

FINISHED: _____

☆ ☆ ☆ ☆ ☆

FORMAT READ: EBOOK / PRINT / AUDIOBOOK

✓ **SYNOPSIS/THINGS I LIKED:**

_____
_____
_____
_____
_____

🚫 **THINGS I DIDN'T LIKE:**

_____
_____
_____
_____
_____

✏️ **FAVORITE QUOTE(S):**

_____
_____
_____
_____
_____
_____
_____
_____

TITLE: _____

GENRE: _____

SERIES: _____

AUTHOR: _____

PAGES: _____

STARTED: _____

FINISHED: _____

☆☆☆☆☆

FORMAT READ: EBOOK / PRINT / AUDIOBOOK

✓ **SYNOPSIS/THINGS I LIKED:**

_____
_____
_____
_____
_____

🚫 **THINGS I DIDN'T LIKE:**

_____
_____
_____
_____
_____

📝 **FAVORITE QUOTE(S):**

_____
_____
_____
_____
_____
_____
_____
_____

✓ SYNOPSIS/THINGS I LIKED:

_____

_____

_____

_____

_____

⊘ THINGS I DIDN'T LIKE:

_____

_____

_____

_____

🖊 FAVORITE QUOTE(S):

_____

_____

_____

_____

_____

_____

_____

TITLE: _____

GENRE: _____

SERIES: _____

AUTHOR: _____

PAGES: _____

STARTED: _____

FINISHED: _____

☆ ☆ ☆ ☆ ☆

FORMAT READ: EBOOK / PRINT / AUDIOBOOK **19**

SYNOPSIS/THINGS I LIKED:

_____

_____

_____

_____

_____

THINGS I DIDN'T LIKE:

_____

_____

_____

_____

FAVORITE QUOTE(S):

_____

_____

_____

_____

_____

_____

_____

TITLE: _____

GENRE: _____

SERIES: _____

AUTHOR: _____

PAGES: _____

STARTED: _____

FINISHED: _____

☆ ☆ ☆ ☆ ☆

FORMAT READ: EBOOK / PRINT / AUDIOBOOK

TITLE: _____

GENRE: _____

SERIES: _____

AUTHOR: _____

PAGES: _____

STARTED: _____

FINISHED: _____

☆ ☆ ☆ ☆ ☆

FORMAT READ: EBOOK / PRINT / AUDIOBOOK

SYNOPSIS/THINGS I LIKED:

_____
_____
_____
_____
_____

THINGS I DIDN'T LIKE:

_____
_____
_____
_____

FAVORITE QUOTE(S):

_____
_____
_____
_____
_____
_____
_____

TITLE: _____

GENRE: _____

SERIES: _____

AUTHOR: _____

PAGES: _____

STARTED: _____

FINISHED: _____

☆ ☆ ☆ ☆ ☆

FORMAT READ: EBOOK / PRINT / AUDIOBOOK

☑ **SYNOPSIS/THINGS I LIKED:** _____

_____

_____

_____

🚫 **THINGS I DIDN'T LIKE:** _____

_____

_____

_____

✎ **FAVORITE QUOTE(S):** _____

_____

_____

_____

_____

_____

_____

✔ **SYNOPSIS/THINGS I LIKED:**

_____
_____
_____
_____
_____

🚫 **THINGS I DIDN'T LIKE:**

_____
_____
_____
_____

✎ **FAVORITE QUOTE(S):**

_____
_____
_____
_____
_____
_____

TITLE: _____

GENRE: _____

SERIES: _____

AUTHOR: _____

PAGES: _____

STARTED: _____

FINISHED: _____

☆ ☆ ☆ ☆ ☆

FORMAT READ: EBOOK / PRINT / AUDIOBOOK **23**

✔ SYNOPSIS/THINGS I LIKED:
_____
_____
_____
_____
_____

🚫 THINGS I DIDN'T LIKE:
_____
_____
_____
_____

✏️ FAVORITE QUOTE(S):
_____
_____
_____
_____
_____
_____
_____

TITLE: _____

GENRE: _____

SERIES: _____

AUTHOR: _____

PAGES: _____

STARTED: _____

FINISHED: _____

☆ ☆ ☆ ☆ ☆

FORMAT READ: EBOOK / PRINT / AUDIOBOOK

TITLE: _____

GENRE: _____

SERIES: _____

AUTHOR: _____

PAGES: _____

STARTED: _____

FINISHED: _____

☆ ☆ ☆ ☆ ☆

FORMAT READ: EBOOK / PRINT / AUDIOBOOK

✓ SYNOPSIS/THINGS I LIKED: _____

_____

_____

_____

_____

🚫 THINGS I DIDN'T LIKE: _____

_____

_____

_____

_____

✎ FAVORITE QUOTE(S): _____

_____

_____

_____

_____

_____

_____

_____

TITLE: _____

GENRE: _____

SERIES: _____

AUTHOR: _____

PAGES: _____

STARTED: _____

FINISHED: _____

☆☆☆☆☆

FORMAT READ: EBOOK / PRINT / AUDIOBOOK

✓ **SYNOPSIS/THINGS I LIKED:**

_____

_____

_____

_____

🚫 **THINGS I DIDN'T LIKE:**

_____

_____

_____

_____

✒ **FAVORITE QUOTE(S):**

_____

_____

_____

_____

_____

_____

☑ **SYNOPSIS/THINGS I LIKED:**

_____
_____
_____
_____
_____
_____

🚫 **THINGS I DIDN'T LIKE:**

_____
_____
_____
_____
_____

📝 **FAVORITE QUOTE(S):**

_____
_____
_____
_____
_____
_____
_____
_____

TITLE: _____

GENRE: _____

SERIES: _____

AUTHOR: _____

PAGES: _____

STARTED: _____

FINISHED: _____

☆ ☆ ☆ ☆ ☆

FORMAT READ: EBOOK / PRINT / AUDIOBOOK **27**

✓ **SYNOPSIS/THINGS I LIKED:**

_____

_____

_____

_____

_____

🚫 **THINGS I DIDN'T LIKE:**

_____

_____

_____

_____

_____

🖍 **FAVORITE QUOTE(S):**

_____

_____

_____

_____

_____

_____

_____

TITLE: _____

GENRE: _____

SERIES: _____

AUTHOR: _____

PAGES: _____

STARTED: _____

FINISHED: _____

☆ ☆ ☆ ☆ ☆

FORMAT READ: EBOOK / PRINT / AUDIOBOOK

TITLE: _____

GENRE: _____

SERIES: _____

AUTHOR: _____

PAGES: _____

STARTED: _____

FINISHED: _____

☆ ☆ ☆ ☆ ☆

FORMAT READ: EBOOK / PRINT / AUDIOBOOK

☑ SYNOPSIS/THINGS I LIKED:

_____

_____

_____

_____

_____

🚫 THINGS I DIDN'T LIKE:

_____

_____

_____

_____

_____

✎ FAVORITE QUOTE(S):

_____

_____

_____

_____

_____

_____

_____

_____

TITLE: _____

GENRE: _____

SERIES: _____

AUTHOR: _____

PAGES: _____

STARTED: _____

FINISHED: _____

☆ ☆ ☆ ☆ ☆

FORMAT READ: EBOOK / PRINT / AUDIOBOOK

✓ **SYNOPSIS/THINGS I LIKED:**

_____
_____
_____
_____
_____

🚫 **THINGS I DIDN'T LIKE:**

_____
_____
_____
_____
_____

✎ **FAVORITE QUOTE(S):**

_____
_____
_____
_____
_____
_____
_____
_____

✓ SYNOPSIS/THINGS I LIKED:

_____

_____

_____

_____

_____

🚫 THINGS I DIDN'T LIKE:

_____

_____

_____

_____

📝 FAVORITE QUOTE(S):

_____

_____

_____

_____

_____

_____

_____

_____

TITLE: _____

GENRE: _____

SERIES: _____

AUTHOR: _____

PAGES: _____

STARTED: _____

FINISHED: _____

☆ ☆ ☆ ☆ ☆

FORMAT READ: EBOOK / PRINT / AUDIOBOOK 31

☑ **SYNOPSIS/THINGS I LIKED:**

_____

_____

_____

_____

_____

🚫 **THINGS I DIDN'T LIKE:**

_____

_____

_____

_____

_____

📝 **FAVORITE QUOTE(S):**

_____

_____

_____

_____

_____

_____

_____

_____

TITLE: _____

GENRE: _____

SERIES: _____

AUTHOR: _____

PAGES: _____

STARTED: _____

FINISHED: _____

☆ ☆ ☆ ☆ ☆

FORMAT READ: EBOOK / PRINT / AUDIOBOOK

TITLE: _____

GENRE: _____

SERIES: _____

AUTHOR: _____

PAGES: _____

STARTED: _____

FINISHED: _____

☆☆☆☆☆

FORMAT READ: EBOOK / PRINT / AUDIOBOOK

✓ **SYNOPSIS/THINGS I LIKED:** _____

_____

_____

_____

_____

🚫 **THINGS I DIDN'T LIKE:** _____

_____

_____

_____

_____

📓 **FAVORITE QUOTE(S):** _____

_____

_____

_____

_____

_____

_____

_____

_____

TITLE: _____

GENRE: _____

SERIES: _____

AUTHOR: _____

PAGES: _____

STARTED: _____

FINISHED: _____

☆ ☆ ☆ ☆ ☆

FORMAT READ: EBOOK / PRINT / AUDIOBOOK

✔ **SYNOPSIS/THINGS I LIKED:**

_____
_____
_____
_____
_____

🚫 **THINGS I DIDN'T LIKE:**

_____
_____
_____
_____

✎ **FAVORITE QUOTE(S):**

_____
_____
_____
_____
_____
_____
_____
_____

✔ **SYNOPSIS/THINGS I LIKED:**

_____
_____
_____
_____

🚫 **THINGS I DIDN'T LIKE:**

_____
_____
_____
_____

✏️ **FAVORITE QUOTE(S):**

_____
_____
_____
_____
_____
_____

TITLE: _____

GENRE: _____

SERIES: _____

AUTHOR: _____

PAGES: _____

STARTED: _____

FINISHED: _____

☆ ☆ ☆ ☆ ☆

☑ **SYNOPSIS/THINGS I LIKED:**

_____
_____
_____
_____
_____

🚫 **THINGS I DIDN'T LIKE:**

_____
_____
_____
_____
_____

✎ **FAVORITE QUOTE(S):**

_____
_____
_____
_____
_____
_____
_____

TITLE: _____

GENRE: _____

SERIES: _____

AUTHOR: _____

PAGES: _____

STARTED: _____

FINISHED: _____

☆ ☆ ☆ ☆ ☆

FORMAT READ: EBOOK / PRINT / AUDIOBOOK

TITLE: _____

GENRE: _____

SERIES: _____

AUTHOR: _____

PAGES: _____

STARTED: _____

FINISHED: _____

☆ ☆ ☆ ☆ ☆

FORMAT READ: EBOOK / PRINT / AUDIOBOOK

✓ SYNOPSIS/THINGS I LIKED:

_____

_____

_____

_____

🚫 THINGS I DIDN'T LIKE:

_____

_____

_____

_____

✎ FAVORITE QUOTE(S):

_____

_____

_____

_____

_____

_____

TITLE: _____

GENRE: _____

SERIES: _____

AUTHOR: _____

PAGES: _____

STARTED: _____

FINISHED: _____

☆☆☆☆☆

FORMAT READ: EBOOK / PRINT / AUDIOBOOK

✓ SYNOPSIS/THINGS I LIKED: _____

_____

_____

_____

_____

🚫 THINGS I DIDN'T LIKE: _____

_____

_____

_____

✏️ FAVORITE QUOTE(S): _____

_____

_____

_____

_____

_____

_____

✓ **SYNOPSIS/THINGS I LIKED:**

_____

_____

_____

_____

🚫 **THINGS I DIDN'T LIKE:**

_____

_____

_____

_____

✏️ **FAVORITE QUOTE(S):**

_____

_____

_____

_____

_____

_____

_____

TITLE: _____

GENRE: _____

SERIES: _____

AUTHOR: _____

PAGES: _____

STARTED: _____

FINISHED: _____

☆ ☆ ☆ ☆ ☆

FORMAT READ: EBOOK / PRINT / AUDIOBOOK 39

✔ **SYNOPSIS/THINGS I LIKED:**

_____

_____

_____

_____

_____

🚫 **THINGS I DIDN'T LIKE:**

_____

_____

_____

_____

_____

📝 **FAVORITE QUOTE(S):**

_____

_____

_____

_____

_____

_____

_____

TITLE: _____

GENRE: _____

SERIES: _____

AUTHOR: _____

PAGES: _____

STARTED: _____

FINISHED: _____

☆ ☆ ☆ ☆ ☆

FORMAT READ: EBOOK / PRINT / AUDIOBOOK

TITLE: _____

GENRE: _____

SERIES: _____

AUTHOR: _____

PAGES: _____

STARTED: _____

FINISHED: _____

☆ ☆ ☆ ☆ ☆

FORMAT READ: EBOOK / PRINT / AUDIOBOOK

SYNOPSIS/THINGS I LIKED:

_____
_____
_____
_____
_____

THINGS I DIDN'T LIKE:

_____
_____
_____
_____

FAVORITE QUOTE(S):

_____
_____
_____
_____
_____
_____
_____

TITLE: _____

GENRE: _____

SERIES: _____

AUTHOR: _____

PAGES: _____

STARTED: _____

FINISHED: _____

☆ ☆ ☆ ☆ ☆

FORMAT READ: EBOOK / PRINT / AUDIOBOOK

☑ **SYNOPSIS/THINGS I LIKED:**

_____
_____
_____
_____

🚫 **THINGS I DIDN'T LIKE:**

_____
_____
_____
_____

✎ **FAVORITE QUOTE(S):**

_____
_____
_____
_____
_____
_____
_____

✔ **SYNOPSIS/THINGS I LIKED:**

_____
_____
_____
_____

🚫 **THINGS I DIDN'T LIKE:**

_____
_____
_____
_____

✎ **FAVORITE QUOTE(S):**

_____
_____
_____
_____
_____
_____

TITLE: _____

GENRE: _____

SERIES: _____

AUTHOR: _____

PAGES: _____

STARTED: _____

FINISHED: _____

☆ ☆ ☆ ☆ ☆

_____

_____

_____

_____

🚫 **THINGS I DIDN'T LIKE:**

_____

_____

_____

_____

📝 **FAVORITE QUOTE(S):**

_____

_____

_____

_____

_____

_____

TITLE: _____

GENRE: _____

SERIES: _____

AUTHOR: _____

PAGES: _____

STARTED: _____

FINISHED: _____

☆ ☆ ☆ ☆ ☆

FORMAT READ: EBOOK / PRINT / AUDIOBOOK

TITLE: _____

GENRE: _____

SERIES: _____

AUTHOR: _____

PAGES: _____

STARTED: _____

FINISHED: _____

☆☆☆☆☆

FORMAT READ: EBOOK / PRINT / AUDIOBOOK

✔ SYNOPSIS/THINGS I LIKED:

_____
_____
_____
_____

🚫 THINGS I DIDN'T LIKE:

_____
_____
_____
_____

✎ FAVORITE QUOTE(S):

_____
_____
_____
_____
_____
_____
_____

TITLE: _____

GENRE: _____

SERIES: _____

AUTHOR: _____

PAGES: _____

STARTED: _____

FINISHED: _____

☆ ☆ ☆ ☆ ☆

FORMAT READ: EBOOK / PRINT / AUDIOBOOK

✓ **SYNOPSIS/THINGS I LIKED:**

_____
_____
_____
_____
_____

🚫 **THINGS I DIDN'T LIKE:**

_____
_____
_____
_____

✎ **FAVORITE QUOTE(S):**

_____
_____
_____
_____
_____
_____
_____

✓ **SYNOPSIS/THINGS I LIKED:**

_____
_____
_____
_____

🚫 **THINGS I DIDN'T LIKE:**

_____
_____
_____
_____

✏️ **FAVORITE QUOTE(S):**

_____
_____
_____
_____
_____
_____

TITLE: _____

GENRE: _____

SERIES: _____

AUTHOR: _____

PAGES: _____

STARTED: _____

FINISHED: _____

☆ ☆ ☆ ☆ ☆

✓ **SYNOPSIS/THINGS I LIKED:**

_____

_____

_____

_____

🚫 **THINGS I DIDN'T LIKE:**

_____

_____

_____

_____

✎ **FAVORITE QUOTE(S):**

_____

_____

_____

_____

_____

_____

_____

TITLE: _____

GENRE: _____

SERIES: _____

AUTHOR: _____

PAGES: _____

STARTED: _____

FINISHED: _____

☆ ☆ ☆ ☆ ☆

FORMAT READ: EBOOK / PRINT / AUDIOBOOK

TITLE: _____

GENRE: _____

SERIES: _____

AUTHOR: _____

PAGES: _____

STARTED: _____

FINISHED: _____

☆ ☆ ☆ ☆ ☆

FORMAT READ: EBOOK / PRINT / AUDIOBOOK

✓ SYNOPSIS/THINGS I LIKED:
_____
_____
_____
_____
_____

🚫 THINGS I DIDN'T LIKE:
_____
_____
_____
_____

✎ FAVORITE QUOTE(S):
_____
_____
_____
_____
_____
_____
_____

TITLE: _____

GENRE: _____

SERIES: _____

AUTHOR: _____

PAGES: _____

STARTED: _____

FINISHED: _____

☆☆☆☆☆

FORMAT READ: EBOOK / PRINT / AUDIOBOOK

✔️ **SYNOPSIS/THINGS I LIKED:**

_____
_____
_____
_____
_____

🚫 **THINGS I DIDN'T LIKE:**

_____
_____
_____
_____
_____

✏️ **FAVORITE QUOTE(S):**

_____
_____
_____
_____
_____
_____
_____

✓ SYNOPSIS/THINGS I LIKED:

_____
_____
_____
_____
_____

🚫 THINGS I DIDN'T LIKE:

_____
_____
_____
_____

✏️ FAVORITE QUOTE(S):

_____
_____
_____
_____
_____
_____
_____

TITLE: _____

GENRE: _____

SERIES: _____

AUTHOR: _____

PAGES: _____

STARTED: _____

FINISHED: _____

☆ ☆ ☆ ☆ ☆

FORMAT READ: EBOOK / PRINT / AUDIOBOOK 51

☑ **Synopsis/Things I liked:**

_____
_____
_____
_____
_____

🚫 **Things I didn't like:**

_____
_____
_____
_____
_____

✎ **Favorite quote(s):**

_____
_____
_____
_____
_____
_____
_____

Title: _____

Genre: _____

Series: _____

Author: _____

Pages: _____

Started: _____

Finished: _____

☆ ☆ ☆ ☆ ☆

Format read: Ebook / Print / Audiobook

TITLE: _____

GENRE: _____

SERIES: _____

AUTHOR: _____

PAGES: _____

STARTED: _____

FINISHED: _____

☆ ☆ ☆ ☆ ☆

FORMAT READ: EBOOK / PRINT / AUDIOBOOK

✔ SYNOPSIS/THINGS I LIKED:

_____

_____

_____

_____

🚫 THINGS I DIDN'T LIKE:

_____

_____

_____

_____

✎ FAVORITE QUOTE(S):

_____

_____

_____

_____

_____

_____

TITLE: _____

GENRE: _____

SERIES: _____

AUTHOR: _____

PAGES: _____

STARTED: _____

FINISHED: _____

☆ ☆ ☆ ☆ ☆

FORMAT READ: EBOOK / PRINT / AUDIOBOOK

✓ **SYNOPSIS/THINGS I LIKED:**

_____
_____
_____
_____

🚫 **THINGS I DIDN'T LIKE:**

_____
_____
_____

✏️ **FAVORITE QUOTE(S):**

_____
_____
_____
_____
_____
_____

✔ **Synopsis/Things I liked:**

_____
_____
_____
_____
_____

🚫 **Things I didn't like:**

_____
_____
_____
_____
_____

✎ **Favorite quote(s):**

_____
_____
_____
_____
_____
_____
_____

Title: _____

Genre: _____

Series: _____

Author: _____

Pages: _____

Started: _____

Finished: _____

☆ ☆ ☆ ☆ ☆

✓ **SYNOPSIS/THINGS I LIKED:**

_____

_____

_____

_____

🚫 **THINGS I DIDN'T LIKE:**

_____

_____

_____

_____

✎ **FAVORITE QUOTE(S):**

_____

_____

_____

_____

_____

_____

TITLE: _____

GENRE: _____

SERIES: _____

AUTHOR: _____

PAGES: _____

STARTED: _____

FINISHED: _____

☆ ☆ ☆ ☆ ☆

FORMAT READ: EBOOK / PRINT / AUDIOBOOK

TITLE: _____

GENRE: _____

SERIES: _____

AUTHOR: _____

PAGES: _____

STARTED: _____

FINISHED: _____

☆☆☆☆☆

FORMAT READ: EBOOK / PRINT / AUDIOBOOK

✓ **SYNOPSIS/THINGS I LIKED:**

_____
_____
_____
_____

🚫 **THINGS I DIDN'T LIKE:**

_____
_____
_____
_____

✍ **FAVORITE QUOTE(S):**

_____
_____
_____
_____
_____
_____
_____

TITLE: _____

GENRE: _____

SERIES: _____

AUTHOR: _____

PAGES: _____

STARTED: _____

FINISHED: _____

☆☆☆☆☆

FORMAT READ: EBOOK / PRINT / AUDIOBOOK

✓ **SYNOPSIS/THINGS I LIKED:**

_____
_____
_____
_____
_____

🚫 **THINGS I DIDN'T LIKE:**

_____
_____
_____
_____

📝 **FAVORITE QUOTE(S):**

_____
_____
_____
_____
_____
_____
_____

✓ **SYNOPSIS/THINGS I LIKED:**

_____

_____

_____

_____

🚫 **THINGS I DIDN'T LIKE:**

_____

_____

_____

_____

📝 **FAVORITE QUOTE(S):**

_____

_____

_____

_____

_____

_____

TITLE: _____

GENRE: _____

SERIES: _____

AUTHOR: _____

PAGES: _____

STARTED: _____

FINISHED: _____

☆☆☆☆☆

✔ SYNOPSIS/THINGS I LIKED:

_____
_____
_____
_____

🚫 THINGS I DIDN'T LIKE:

_____
_____
_____
_____

✎ FAVORITE QUOTE(S):

_____
_____
_____
_____
_____
_____
_____

TITLE: _____

GENRE: _____

SERIES: _____

AUTHOR: _____

PAGES: _____

STARTED: _____

FINISHED: _____

☆ ☆ ☆ ☆ ☆

FORMAT READ: EBOOK / PRINT / AUDIOBOOK

TITLE: _____

GENRE: _____

SERIES: _____

AUTHOR: _____

PAGES: _____

STARTED: _____

FINISHED: _____

☆☆☆☆☆

FORMAT READ: EBOOK / PRINT / AUDIOBOOK

✓ SYNOPSIS/THINGS I LIKED:
_____
_____
_____
_____

🚫 THINGS I DIDN'T LIKE:
_____
_____
_____
_____

✏️ FAVORITE QUOTE(S):
_____
_____
_____
_____
_____
_____
_____

TITLE: _____

GENRE: _____

SERIES: _____

AUTHOR: _____

PAGES: _____

STARTED: _____

FINISHED: _____

☆☆☆☆☆

FORMAT READ: EBOOK / PRINT / AUDIOBOOK

✓ SYNOPSIS/THINGS I LIKED:
_____
_____
_____
_____
_____

🚫 THINGS I DIDN'T LIKE:
_____
_____
_____
_____

✎ FAVORITE QUOTE(S):
_____
_____
_____
_____
_____
_____
_____

✓ **Synopsis/Things I liked:**

_____
_____
_____
_____
_____

🚫 **Things I didn't like:**

_____
_____
_____
_____

✏️ **Favorite quote(s):**

_____
_____
_____
_____
_____
_____
_____

Title: _____

Genre: _____

Series: _____

Author: _____

Pages: _____

Started: _____

Finished: _____

☆ ☆ ☆ ☆ ☆

✓ **SYNOPSIS/THINGS I LIKED:**

_____

_____

_____

_____

🚫 **THINGS I DIDN'T LIKE:**

_____

_____

_____

_____

✎ **FAVORITE QUOTE(S):**

_____

_____

_____

_____

_____

_____

TITLE: _____

GENRE: _____

SERIES: _____

AUTHOR: _____

PAGES: _____

STARTED: _____

FINISHED: _____

☆ ☆ ☆ ☆ ☆

FORMAT READ: EBOOK / PRINT / AUDIOBOOK

TITLE: _____

GENRE: _____

SERIES: _____

AUTHOR: _____

PAGES: _____

STARTED: _____

FINISHED: _____

☆☆☆☆☆

FORMAT READ: EBOOK / PRINT / AUDIOBOOK

✓ SYNOPSIS/THINGS I LIKED:
_____
_____
_____
_____

🚫 THINGS I DIDN'T LIKE:
_____
_____
_____
_____

✏ FAVORITE QUOTE(S):
_____
_____
_____
_____
_____
_____
_____
_____

TITLE: _____

GENRE: _____

SERIES: _____

AUTHOR: _____

PAGES: _____

STARTED: _____

FINISHED: _____

☆☆☆☆☆

FORMAT READ: EBOOK / PRINT / AUDIOBOOK

✓ **SYNOPSIS/THINGS I LIKED:**

_____
_____
_____
_____

🚫 **THINGS I DIDN'T LIKE:**

_____
_____
_____
_____

✏️ **FAVORITE QUOTE(S):**

_____
_____
_____
_____
_____
_____
_____
_____

✅ **SYNOPSIS/THINGS I LIKED:**

_____
_____
_____
_____
_____

🚫 **THINGS I DIDN'T LIKE:**

_____
_____
_____
_____
_____

✏️ **FAVORITE QUOTE(S):**

_____
_____
_____
_____
_____
_____
_____

TITLE: _____

GENRE: _____

SERIES: _____

AUTHOR: _____

PAGES: _____

STARTED: _____

FINISHED: _____

☆ ☆ ☆ ☆ ☆

✓ **SYNOPSIS/THINGS I LIKED:**

_____

_____

_____

_____

_____

🚫 **THINGS I DIDN'T LIKE:**

_____

_____

_____

_____

_____

✎ **FAVORITE QUOTE(S):**

_____

_____

_____

_____

_____

_____

_____

TITLE: _____

GENRE: _____

SERIES: _____

AUTHOR: _____

PAGES: _____

STARTED: _____

FINISHED: _____

☆ ☆ ☆ ☆ ☆

FORMAT READ: EBOOK / PRINT / AUDIOBOOK

TITLE: _____

GENRE: _____

SERIES: _____

AUTHOR: _____

PAGES: _____

STARTED: _____

FINISHED: _____

☆ ☆ ☆ ☆ ☆

FORMAT READ: EBOOK / PRINT / AUDIOBOOK

✓ **SYNOPSIS/THINGS I LIKED:**

_____
_____
_____
_____

🚫 **THINGS I DIDN'T LIKE:**

_____
_____
_____
_____

✏️ **FAVORITE QUOTE(S):**

_____
_____
_____
_____
_____
_____
_____
_____

TITLE: _____

GENRE: _____

SERIES: _____

AUTHOR: _____

PAGES: _____

STARTED: _____

FINISHED: _____

☆ ☆ ☆ ☆ ☆

FORMAT READ: EBOOK / PRINT / AUDIOBOOK

☑ **SYNOPSIS/THINGS I LIKED:**

_____
_____
_____
_____

🚫 **THINGS I DIDN'T LIKE:**

_____
_____
_____
_____

✏️ **FAVORITE QUOTE(S):**

_____
_____
_____
_____
_____
_____

✔ **SYNOPSIS/THINGS I LIKED:**

_____
_____
_____
_____

🚫 **THINGS I DIDN'T LIKE:**

_____
_____
_____
_____

✎ **FAVORITE QUOTE(S):**

_____
_____
_____
_____
_____
_____

TITLE: _____

GENRE: _____

SERIES: _____

AUTHOR: _____

PAGES: _____

STARTED: _____

FINISHED: _____

☆☆☆☆☆

✓ **Synopsis/Things I liked:**

_____

_____

_____

_____

_____

🚫 **Things I didn't like:**

_____

_____

_____

_____

✎ **Favorite quote(s):**

_____

_____

_____

_____

_____

_____

_____

Title: _____

Genre: _____

Series: _____

Author: _____

Pages: _____

Started: _____

Finished: _____

☆ ☆ ☆ ☆ ☆

Format read: Ebook / Print / Audiobook

TITLE: _____

GENRE: _____

SERIES: _____

AUTHOR: _____

PAGES: _____

STARTED: _____

FINISHED: _____

☆☆☆☆☆

FORMAT READ: EBOOK / PRINT / AUDIOBOOK

✅ SYNOPSIS/THINGS I LIKED: _____
_____
_____
_____
_____

🚫 THINGS I DIDN'T LIKE: _____
_____
_____
_____
_____

✏️ FAVORITE QUOTE(S): _____
_____
_____
_____
_____
_____
_____
_____

TITLE: _____

GENRE: _____

SERIES: _____

AUTHOR: _____

PAGES: _____

STARTED: _____

FINISHED: _____

☆ ☆ ☆ ☆ ☆

FORMAT READ: EBOOK / PRINT / AUDIOBOOK

✓ **SYNOPSIS/THINGS I LIKED:**

_____
_____
_____
_____

🚫 **THINGS I DIDN'T LIKE:**

_____
_____
_____
_____

✎ **FAVORITE QUOTE(S):**

_____
_____
_____
_____
_____
_____
_____

✅ **SYNOPSIS/THINGS I LIKED:**

_____

_____

_____

_____

🚫 **THINGS I DIDN'T LIKE:**

_____

_____

_____

_____

✏️ **FAVORITE QUOTE(S):**

_____

_____

_____

_____

_____

_____

_____

TITLE: _____

GENRE: _____

SERIES: _____

AUTHOR: _____

PAGES: _____

STARTED: _____

FINISHED: _____

☆ ☆ ☆ ☆ ☆

☑ **SYNOPSIS/THINGS I LIKED:**

_____
_____
_____
_____

🚫 **THINGS I DIDN'T LIKE:**

_____
_____
_____
_____

📝 **FAVORITE QUOTE(S):**

_____
_____
_____
_____
_____
_____

TITLE: _____

GENRE: _____

SERIES: _____

AUTHOR: _____

PAGES: _____

STARTED: _____

FINISHED: _____

☆ ☆ ☆ ☆ ☆

FORMAT READ: EBOOK / PRINT / AUDIOBOOK

TITLE: _____

GENRE: _____

SERIES: _____

AUTHOR: _____

PAGES: _____

STARTED: _____

FINISHED: _____

☆ ☆ ☆ ☆ ☆

FORMAT READ: EBOOK / PRINT / AUDIOBOOK

✓ SYNOPSIS/THINGS I LIKED: _____

_____

_____

_____

_____

🚫 THINGS I DIDN'T LIKE: _____

_____

_____

_____

_____

📝 FAVORITE QUOTE(S): _____

_____

_____

_____

_____

_____

_____

_____

TITLE: _____

GENRE: _____

SERIES: _____

AUTHOR: _____

PAGES: _____

STARTED: _____

FINISHED: _____

☆☆☆☆☆

FORMAT READ: EBOOK / PRINT / AUDIOBOOK

✓ SYNOPSIS/THINGS I LIKED: _____

_____

_____

_____

_____

🚫 THINGS I DIDN'T LIKE: _____

_____

_____

_____

_____

✎ FAVORITE QUOTE(S): _____

_____

_____

_____

_____

_____

_____

_____

✔ **SYNOPSIS/THINGS I LIKED:**

_____
_____
_____
_____

🚫 **THINGS I DIDN'T LIKE:**

_____
_____
_____
_____

📝 **FAVORITE QUOTE(S):**

_____
_____
_____
_____
_____
_____

TITLE: _____

GENRE: _____

SERIES: _____

AUTHOR: _____

PAGES: _____

STARTED: _____

FINISHED: _____

☆ ☆ ☆ ☆ ☆

✓ **SYNOPSIS/THINGS I LIKED:**

_____
_____
_____
_____

🚫 **THINGS I DIDN'T LIKE:**

_____
_____
_____
_____

✎ **FAVORITE QUOTE(S):**

_____
_____
_____
_____
_____
_____

TITLE: _____

GENRE: _____

SERIES: _____

AUTHOR: _____

PAGES: _____

STARTED: _____

FINISHED: _____

☆ ☆ ☆ ☆ ☆

FORMAT READ: EBOOK / PRINT / AUDIOBOOK

TITLE: _____

GENRE: _____

SERIES: _____

AUTHOR: _____

PAGES: _____

STARTED: _____

FINISHED: _____

☆☆☆☆☆

FORMAT READ: EBOOK / PRINT / AUDIOBOOK

SYNOPSIS/THINGS I LIKED:

_____
_____
_____
_____

THINGS I DIDN'T LIKE:

_____
_____
_____
_____

FAVORITE QUOTE(S):

_____
_____
_____
_____
_____
_____
_____

TITLE: _____

GENRE: _____

SERIES: _____

AUTHOR: _____

PAGES: _____

STARTED: _____

FINISHED: _____

☆ ☆ ☆ ☆ ☆

FORMAT READ: EBOOK / PRINT / AUDIOBOOK

☑ **SYNOPSIS/THINGS I LIKED:**

_____
_____
_____
_____

🚫 **THINGS I DIDN'T LIKE:**

_____
_____
_____
_____

✏ **FAVORITE QUOTE(S):**

_____
_____
_____
_____
_____
_____

✅ **SYNOPSIS/THINGS I LIKED:**

_____

_____

_____

_____

🚫 **THINGS I DIDN'T LIKE:**

_____

_____

_____

_____

📝 **FAVORITE QUOTE(S):**

_____

_____

_____

_____

_____

_____

TITLE: _____

GENRE: _____

SERIES: _____

AUTHOR: _____

PAGES: _____

STARTED: _____

FINISHED: _____

☆ ☆ ☆ ☆ ☆

✅ **SYNOPSIS/THINGS I LIKED:**

_____
_____
_____
_____

🚫 **THINGS I DIDN'T LIKE:**

_____
_____
_____
_____

📝 **FAVORITE QUOTE(S):**

_____
_____
_____
_____
_____
_____
_____

TITLE: _____

GENRE: _____

SERIES: _____

AUTHOR: _____

PAGES: _____

STARTED: _____

FINISHED: _____

☆ ☆ ☆ ☆ ☆

FORMAT READ: EBOOK / PRINT / AUDIOBOOK

TITLE: _____

GENRE: _____

SERIES: _____

AUTHOR: _____

PAGES: _____

STARTED: _____

FINISHED: _____

☆☆☆☆☆

FORMAT READ: EBOOK / PRINT / AUDIOBOOK

✓ SYNOPSIS/THINGS I LIKED:
_____
_____
_____
_____

🚫 THINGS I DIDN'T LIKE:
_____
_____
_____
_____

✎ FAVORITE QUOTE(S):
_____
_____
_____
_____
_____
_____
_____
_____

TITLE: _____

GENRE: _____

SERIES: _____

AUTHOR: _____

PAGES: _____

STARTED: _____

FINISHED: _____

☆☆☆☆☆

FORMAT READ: EBOOK / PRINT / AUDIOBOOK

☑ **SYNOPSIS/THINGS I LIKED:**

_____
_____
_____
_____
_____

🚫 **THINGS I DIDN'T LIKE:**

_____
_____
_____
_____

✎ **FAVORITE QUOTE(S):**

_____
_____
_____
_____
_____
_____
_____

✔ **Synopsis/Things I liked:**

_____
_____
_____
_____

🚫 **Things I didn't like:**

_____
_____
_____
_____

✏ **Favorite quote(s):**

_____
_____
_____
_____
_____
_____
_____

Title: _____

Genre: _____

Series: _____

Author: _____

Pages: _____

Started: _____

Finished: _____

☆ ☆ ☆ ☆ ☆

✓ **SYNOPSIS/THINGS I LIKED:**

_____

_____

_____

_____

⊘ **THINGS I DIDN'T LIKE:**

_____

_____

_____

_____

✎ **FAVORITE QUOTE(S):**

_____

_____

_____

_____

_____

_____

TITLE: _____

GENRE: _____

SERIES: _____

AUTHOR: _____

PAGES: _____

STARTED: _____

FINISHED: _____

☆ ☆ ☆ ☆ ☆

FORMAT READ: EBOOK / PRINT / AUDIOBOOK

TITLE: _____

GENRE: _____

SERIES: _____

AUTHOR: _____

PAGES: _____

STARTED: _____

FINISHED: _____

☆ ☆ ☆ ☆ ☆

FORMAT READ: EBOOK / PRINT / AUDIOBOOK

✓ SYNOPSIS/THINGS I LIKED:

_____
_____
_____
_____
_____

🚫 THINGS I DIDN'T LIKE:

_____
_____
_____
_____

✏️ FAVORITE QUOTE(S):

_____
_____
_____
_____
_____
_____
_____

TITLE: _____

GENRE: _____

SERIES: _____

AUTHOR: _____

PAGES: _____

STARTED: _____

FINISHED: _____

☆☆☆☆☆

FORMAT READ: EBOOK / PRINT / AUDIOBOOK

✓ **SYNOPSIS/THINGS I LIKED:**

_____
_____
_____
_____

🚫 **THINGS I DIDN'T LIKE:**

_____
_____
_____
_____

✎ **FAVORITE QUOTE(S):**

_____
_____
_____
_____
_____
_____

☑ **SYNOPSIS/THINGS I LIKED:**

_____

_____

_____

_____

🚫 **THINGS I DIDN'T LIKE:**

_____

_____

_____

_____

📝 **FAVORITE QUOTE(S):**

_____

_____

_____

_____

_____

_____

TITLE: _____

GENRE: _____

SERIES: _____

AUTHOR: _____

PAGES: _____

STARTED: _____

FINISHED: _____

☆ ☆ ☆ ☆ ☆

FORMAT READ: EBOOK / PRINT / AUDIOBOOK 91

✓ **SYNOPSIS/THINGS I LIKED:**

_____

_____

_____

_____

🚫 **THINGS I DIDN'T LIKE:**

_____

_____

_____

_____

✏️ **FAVORITE QUOTE(S):**

_____

_____

_____

_____

_____

_____

TITLE: _____

GENRE: _____

SERIES: _____

AUTHOR: _____

PAGES: _____

STARTED: _____

FINISHED: _____

☆ ☆ ☆ ☆ ☆

FORMAT READ: EBOOK / PRINT / AUDIOBOOK

TITLE: _____

GENRE: _____

SERIES: _____

AUTHOR: _____

PAGES: _____

STARTED: _____

FINISHED: _____

☆☆☆☆☆

FORMAT READ: EBOOK / PRINT / AUDIOBOOK

✔ SYNOPSIS/THINGS I LIKED:

_____
_____
_____
_____

🚫 THINGS I DIDN'T LIKE:

_____
_____
_____
_____

✐ FAVORITE QUOTE(S):

_____
_____
_____
_____
_____
_____
_____

TITLE: _____

GENRE: _____

SERIES: _____

AUTHOR: _____

PAGES: _____

STARTED: _____

FINISHED: _____

☆☆☆☆☆

FORMAT READ: EBOOK / PRINT / AUDIOBOOK

✓ **SYNOPSIS/THINGS I LIKED:**

_____

_____

_____

_____

🚫 **THINGS I DIDN'T LIKE:**

_____

_____

_____

✎ **FAVORITE QUOTE(S):**

_____

_____

_____

_____

_____

_____

✓ **SYNOPSIS/THINGS I LIKED:**

_____
_____
_____
_____

🚫 **THINGS I DIDN'T LIKE:**

_____
_____
_____
_____

✏️ **FAVORITE QUOTE(S):**

_____
_____
_____
_____
_____
_____

TITLE: _____

GENRE: _____

SERIES: _____

AUTHOR: _____

PAGES: _____

STARTED: _____

FINISHED: _____

☆ ☆ ☆ ☆ ☆

✓ **SYNOPSIS/THINGS I LIKED:**

_____
_____
_____
_____
_____

🚫 **THINGS I DIDN'T LIKE:**

_____
_____
_____
_____

✎ **FAVORITE QUOTE(S):**

_____
_____
_____
_____
_____
_____
_____

TITLE: _____

GENRE: _____

SERIES: _____

AUTHOR: _____

PAGES: _____

STARTED: _____

FINISHED: _____

☆ ☆ ☆ ☆ ☆

FORMAT READ: EBOOK / PRINT / AUDIOBOOK

TITLE: _____

GENRE: _____

SERIES: _____

AUTHOR: _____

PAGES: _____

STARTED: _____

FINISHED: _____

☆☆☆☆☆

FORMAT READ: EBOOK / PRINT / AUDIOBOOK

✔ SYNOPSIS/THINGS I LIKED:

_____
_____
_____
_____

🚫 THINGS I DIDN'T LIKE:

_____
_____
_____
_____

✎ FAVORITE QUOTE(S):

_____
_____
_____
_____
_____
_____
_____

TITLE: _____

GENRE: _____

SERIES: _____

AUTHOR: _____

PAGES: _____

STARTED: _____

FINISHED: _____

☆☆☆☆☆

FORMAT READ: EBOOK / PRINT / AUDIOBOOK

✓ **SYNOPSIS/THINGS I LIKED:**

_____
_____
_____
_____
_____

🚫 **THINGS I DIDN'T LIKE:**

_____
_____
_____
_____
_____

✒️ **FAVORITE QUOTE(S):**

_____
_____
_____
_____
_____
_____
_____
_____

✔ SYNOPSIS/THINGS I LIKED: _____

_____

_____

_____

_____

🚫 THINGS I DIDN'T LIKE: _____

_____

_____

_____

_____

📝 FAVORITE QUOTE(S): _____

_____

_____

_____

_____

_____

_____

_____

TITLE: _____

GENRE: _____

SERIES: _____

AUTHOR: _____

PAGES: _____

STARTED: _____

FINISHED: _____

☆ ☆ ☆ ☆ ☆

✔ **SYNOPSIS/THINGS I LIKED:**

_____
_____
_____
_____
_____

🚫 **THINGS I DIDN'T LIKE:**

_____
_____
_____
_____
_____

✎ **FAVORITE QUOTE(S):**

_____
_____
_____
_____
_____
_____

TITLE: _____

GENRE: _____

SERIES: _____

AUTHOR: _____

PAGES: _____

STARTED: _____

FINISHED: _____

☆ ☆ ☆ ☆ ☆

FORMAT READ: EBOOK / PRINT / AUDIOBOOK

TITLE: _____

GENRE: _____

SERIES: _____

AUTHOR: _____

PAGES: _____

STARTED: _____

FINISHED: _____

☆ ☆ ☆ ☆ ☆

FORMAT READ: EBOOK / PRINT / AUDIOBOOK

✓ **SYNOPSIS/THINGS I LIKED:**

_____
_____
_____
_____
_____

🚫 **THINGS I DIDN'T LIKE:**

_____
_____
_____
_____

✏️ **FAVORITE QUOTE(S):**

_____
_____
_____
_____
_____
_____
_____

TITLE: _____

GENRE: _____

SERIES: _____

AUTHOR: _____

PAGES: _____

STARTED: _____

FINISHED: _____

☆☆☆☆☆

FORMAT READ: EBOOK / PRINT / AUDIOBOOK

✅ **SYNOPSIS/THINGS I LIKED:** _____

_____

_____

_____

🚫 **THINGS I DIDN'T LIKE:** _____

_____

_____

_____

✏️ **FAVORITE QUOTE(S):** _____

_____

_____

_____

_____

_____

☑ **SYNOPSIS/THINGS I LIKED:**

_____
_____
_____
_____
_____

🚫 **THINGS I DIDN'T LIKE:**

_____
_____
_____
_____

✎ **FAVORITE QUOTE(S):**

_____
_____
_____
_____
_____
_____

TITLE: _____

GENRE: _____

SERIES: _____

AUTHOR: _____

PAGES: _____

STARTED: _____

FINISHED: _____

☆ ☆ ☆ ☆ ☆

FORMAT READ: EBOOK / PRINT / AUDIOBOOK

☑ **SYNOPSIS/THINGS I LIKED:**

_____
_____
_____
_____
_____

🚫 **THINGS I DIDN'T LIKE:**

_____
_____
_____
_____
_____

🖊 **FAVORITE QUOTE(S):**

_____
_____
_____
_____
_____
_____
_____

TITLE: _____

GENRE: _____

SERIES: _____

AUTHOR: _____

PAGES: _____

STARTED: _____

FINISHED: _____

☆ ☆ ☆ ☆ ☆

FORMAT READ: EBOOK / PRINT / AUDIOBOOK

TITLE: _____

GENRE: _____

SERIES: _____

AUTHOR: _____

PAGES: _____

STARTED: _____

FINISHED: _____

☆☆☆☆☆

FORMAT READ: EBOOK / PRINT / AUDIOBOOK

✔️ **SYNOPSIS/THINGS I LIKED:**

_____
_____
_____
_____

🚫 **THINGS I DIDN'T LIKE:**

_____
_____
_____
_____

✏️ **FAVORITE QUOTE(S):**

_____
_____
_____
_____
_____
_____
_____

TITLE: _____

GENRE: _____

SERIES: _____

AUTHOR: _____

PAGES: _____

STARTED: _____

FINISHED: _____

☆ ☆ ☆ ☆ ☆

FORMAT READ: EBOOK / PRINT / AUDIOBOOK

✓ SYNOPSIS/THINGS I LIKED:

_____
_____
_____
_____
_____

🚫 THINGS I DIDN'T LIKE:

_____
_____
_____
_____

✎ FAVORITE QUOTE(S):

_____
_____
_____
_____
_____
_____
_____
_____

☑ **SYNOPSIS/THINGS I LIKED:**

_____
_____
_____
_____

🚫 **THINGS I DIDN'T LIKE:**

_____
_____
_____
_____

✏️ **FAVORITE QUOTE(S):**

_____
_____
_____
_____
_____
_____

TITLE: _____

GENRE: _____

SERIES: _____

AUTHOR: _____

PAGES: _____

STARTED: _____

FINISHED: _____

☆☆☆☆☆

FORMAT READ: EBOOK / PRINT / AUDIOBOOK

107

_____
_____
_____
_____
_____

🚫 THINGS I DIDN'T LIKE:

_____
_____
_____
_____
_____

✏️ FAVORITE QUOTE(S):

_____
_____
_____
_____
_____
_____
_____
_____

TITLE: _____

GENRE: _____

SERIES: _____

AUTHOR: _____

PAGES: _____

STARTED: _____

FINISHED: _____

☆ ☆ ☆ ☆ ☆

FORMAT READ: EBOOK / PRINT / AUDIOBOOK

TITLE: _____

GENRE: _____

SERIES: _____

AUTHOR: _____

PAGES: _____

STARTED: _____

FINISHED: _____

☆ ☆ ☆ ☆ ☆

FORMAT READ: EBOOK / PRINT / AUDIOBOOK

✓ SYNOPSIS/THINGS I LIKED: _____
_____
_____
_____
_____

🚫 THINGS I DIDN'T LIKE: _____
_____
_____
_____
_____

✎ FAVORITE QUOTE(S): _____
_____
_____
_____
_____
_____
_____
_____

TITLE: _____

GENRE: _____

SERIES: _____

AUTHOR: _____

PAGES: _____

STARTED: _____

FINISHED: _____

☆ ☆ ☆ ☆ ☆

FORMAT READ: EBOOK / PRINT / AUDIOBOOK

✓ SYNOPSIS/THINGS I LIKED: _____

_____
_____
_____
_____

🚫 THINGS I DIDN'T LIKE: _____

_____
_____
_____
_____

✎ FAVORITE QUOTE(S): _____

_____
_____
_____
_____
_____
_____

✓ **SYNOPSIS/THINGS I LIKED:**

_____
_____
_____
_____

🚫 **THINGS I DIDN'T LIKE:**

_____
_____
_____
_____

📝 **FAVORITE QUOTE(S):**

_____
_____
_____
_____
_____
_____
_____

TITLE: _____

GENRE: _____

SERIES: _____

AUTHOR: _____

PAGES: _____

STARTED: _____

FINISHED: _____

☆ ☆ ☆ ☆ ☆

FORMAT READ: EBOOK / PRINT / AUDIOBOOK

☑ **SYNOPSIS/THINGS I LIKED:**

_____
_____
_____
_____
_____

🚫 **THINGS I DIDN'T LIKE:**

_____
_____
_____
_____

✎ **FAVORITE QUOTE(S):**

_____
_____
_____
_____
_____
_____
_____

TITLE: _____

GENRE: _____

SERIES: _____

AUTHOR: _____

PAGES: _____

STARTED: _____

FINISHED: _____

☆ ☆ ☆ ☆ ☆

FORMAT READ: EBOOK / PRINT / AUDIOBOOK

TITLE: _____

GENRE: _____

SERIES: _____

AUTHOR: _____

PAGES: _____

STARTED: _____

FINISHED: _____

☆ ☆ ☆ ☆ ☆

FORMAT READ: EBOOK / PRINT / AUDIOBOOK

✓ **SYNOPSIS/THINGS I LIKED:**

_____
_____
_____
_____
_____

🚫 **THINGS I DIDN'T LIKE:**

_____
_____
_____
_____
_____

✏️ **FAVORITE QUOTE(S):**

_____
_____
_____
_____
_____
_____
_____
_____

TITLE: _____

GENRE: _____

SERIES: _____

AUTHOR: _____

PAGES: _____

STARTED: _____

FINISHED: _____

☆☆☆☆☆

FORMAT READ: EBOOK / PRINT / AUDIOBOOK

✓ **SYNOPSIS/THINGS I LIKED:**

_____
_____
_____
_____

🚫 **THINGS I DIDN'T LIKE:**

_____
_____
_____
_____

✏️ **FAVORITE QUOTE(S):**

_____
_____
_____
_____
_____
_____
_____

✔ **SYNOPSIS/THINGS I LIKED:**

_____
_____
_____
_____

🚫 **THINGS I DIDN'T LIKE:**

_____
_____
_____
_____

📝 **FAVORITE QUOTE(S):**

_____
_____
_____
_____
_____
_____

TITLE: _____

GENRE: _____

SERIES: _____

AUTHOR: _____

PAGES: _____

STARTED: _____

FINISHED: _____

☆ ☆ ☆ ☆ ☆

FORMAT READ: EBOOK / PRINT / AUDIOBOOK

115

TITLE: _____

GENRE: _____

SERIES: _____

AUTHOR: _____

PAGES: _____

STARTED: _____

FINISHED: _____

☆ ☆ ☆ ☆ ☆

FORMAT READ: EBOOK / PRINT / AUDIOBOOK

✔ **SYNOPSIS/THINGS I LIKED:**

_____
_____
_____
_____

🚫 **THINGS I DIDN'T LIKE:**

_____
_____
_____
_____

📝 **FAVORITE QUOTE(S):**

_____
_____
_____
_____
_____
_____
_____

TITLE: _____

GENRE: _____

SERIES: _____

AUTHOR: _____

PAGES: _____

STARTED: _____

FINISHED: _____

☆☆☆☆☆

FORMAT READ: EBOOK / PRINT / AUDIOBOOK

✓ **SYNOPSIS/THINGS I LIKED:**

_____

_____

_____

_____

🚫 **THINGS I DIDN'T LIKE:**

_____

_____

_____

_____

✎ **FAVORITE QUOTE(S):**

_____

_____

_____

_____

_____

_____

✓ **SYNOPSIS/THINGS I LIKED:**

_____
_____
_____
_____

🚫 **THINGS I DIDN'T LIKE:**

_____
_____
_____
_____

✏️ **FAVORITE QUOTE(S):**

_____
_____
_____
_____
_____
_____

TITLE: _____

GENRE: _____

SERIES: _____

AUTHOR: _____

PAGES: _____

STARTED: _____

FINISHED: _____

☆☆☆☆☆

FORMAT READ: EBOOK / PRINT / AUDIOBOOK

119

✓ SYNOPSIS/THINGS I LIKED:

_____
_____
_____
_____

🚫 THINGS I DIDN'T LIKE:

_____
_____
_____
_____

✎ FAVORITE QUOTE(S):

_____
_____
_____
_____
_____
_____

TITLE: _____

GENRE: _____

SERIES: _____

AUTHOR: _____

PAGES: _____

STARTED: _____

FINISHED: _____

☆ ☆ ☆ ☆ ☆

FORMAT READ: EBOOK / PRINT / AUDIOBOOK

TITLE: _____

GENRE: _____

SERIES: _____

AUTHOR: _____

PAGES: _____

STARTED: _____

FINISHED: _____

☆ ☆ ☆ ☆ ☆

FORMAT READ: EBOOK / PRINT / AUDIOBOOK

✔ **SYNOPSIS/THINGS I LIKED:**

_____

_____

_____

_____

🚫 **THINGS I DIDN'T LIKE:**

_____

_____

_____

_____

📝 **FAVORITE QUOTE(S):**

_____

_____

_____

_____

_____

_____

TITLE: _____

GENRE: _____

SERIES: _____

AUTHOR: _____

PAGES: _____

STARTED: _____

FINISHED: _____

☆ ☆ ☆ ☆ ☆

FORMAT READ: EBOOK / PRINT / AUDIOBOOK

✔ **SYNOPSIS/THINGS I LIKED:**

_____
_____
_____
_____
_____

🚫 **THINGS I DIDN'T LIKE:**

_____
_____
_____
_____

✏️ **FAVORITE QUOTE(S):**

_____
_____
_____
_____
_____
_____
_____

_____

_____

_____

_____

🚫 THINGS I DIDN'T LIKE:

_____

_____

_____

_____

✎ FAVORITE QUOTE(S):

_____

_____

_____

_____

_____

_____

TITLE: _____

GENRE: _____

SERIES: _____

AUTHOR: _____

PAGES: _____

STARTED: _____

FINISHED: _____

☆ ☆ ☆ ☆ ☆

FORMAT READ: EBOOK / PRINT / AUDIOBOOK

✓ **SYNOPSIS/THINGS I LIKED:**

_____

_____

_____

_____

🚫 **THINGS I DIDN'T LIKE:**

_____

_____

_____

_____

✎ **FAVORITE QUOTE(S):**

_____

_____

_____

_____

_____

_____

TITLE: _____

GENRE: _____

SERIES: _____

AUTHOR: _____

PAGES: _____

STARTED: _____

FINISHED: _____

☆ ☆ ☆ ☆ ☆

FORMAT READ: EBOOK / PRINT / AUDIOBOOK

TITLE: _____

GENRE: _____

SERIES: _____

AUTHOR: _____

PAGES: _____

STARTED: _____

FINISHED: _____

☆☆☆☆☆

FORMAT READ: EBOOK / PRINT / AUDIOBOOK

✓ SYNOPSIS/THINGS I LIKED:

_____
_____
_____
_____
_____

🚫 THINGS I DIDN'T LIKE:

_____
_____
_____
_____
_____

✏️ FAVORITE QUOTE(S):

_____
_____
_____
_____
_____
_____
_____
_____

TITLE: _____

GENRE: _____

SERIES: _____

AUTHOR: _____

PAGES: _____

STARTED: _____

FINISHED: _____

☆ ☆ ☆ ☆ ☆

FORMAT READ: EBOOK / PRINT / AUDIOBOOK

✓ **SYNOPSIS/THINGS I LIKED:**

_____
_____
_____
_____

🚫 **THINGS I DIDN'T LIKE:**

_____
_____
_____
_____

✎ **FAVORITE QUOTE(S):**

_____
_____
_____
_____
_____
_____
_____

✓ **SYNOPSIS/THINGS I LIKED:**

_____
_____
_____
_____

🚫 **THINGS I DIDN'T LIKE:**

_____
_____
_____
_____

📝 **FAVORITE QUOTE(S):**

_____
_____
_____
_____
_____
_____

TITLE: _____

GENRE: _____

SERIES: _____

AUTHOR: _____

PAGES: _____

STARTED: _____

FINISHED: _____

☆ ☆ ☆ ☆ ☆

FORMAT READ: EBOOK / PRINT / AUDIOBOOK

127

☑ **Synopsis/Things I liked:**

_____
_____
_____
_____
_____

🚫 **Things I didn't like:**

_____
_____
_____
_____

✎ **Favorite quote(s):**

_____
_____
_____
_____
_____
_____

Title: _____

Genre: _____

Series: _____

Author: _____

Pages: _____

Started: _____

Finished: _____

☆ ☆ ☆ ☆ ☆

Format read: Ebook / Print / Audiobook

TITLE: _____

GENRE: _____

SERIES: _____

AUTHOR: _____

PAGES: _____

STARTED: _____

FINISHED: _____

☆ ☆ ☆ ☆ ☆

FORMAT READ: EBOOK / PRINT / AUDIOBOOK

✓ **SYNOPSIS/THINGS I LIKED:**

_____
_____
_____
_____

🚫 **THINGS I DIDN'T LIKE:**

_____
_____
_____
_____

✏️ **FAVORITE QUOTE(S):**

_____
_____
_____
_____
_____
_____

TITLE: _____

GENRE: _____

SERIES: _____

AUTHOR: _____

PAGES: _____

STARTED: _____

FINISHED: _____

☆ ☆ ☆ ☆ ☆

FORMAT READ: EBOOK / PRINT / AUDIOBOOK

☑ **SYNOPSIS/THINGS I LIKED:**

_____
_____
_____
_____
_____

🚫 **THINGS I DIDN'T LIKE:**

_____
_____
_____
_____

✏️ **FAVORITE QUOTE(S):**

_____
_____
_____
_____
_____
_____
_____

✓ **SYNOPSIS/THINGS I LIKED:**

_____

_____

_____

_____

_____

🚫 **THINGS I DIDN'T LIKE:**

_____

_____

_____

_____

📝 **FAVORITE QUOTE(S):**

_____

_____

_____

_____

_____

_____

TITLE: _____

GENRE: _____

SERIES: _____

AUTHOR: _____

PAGES: _____

STARTED: _____

FINISHED: _____

☆ ☆ ☆ ☆ ☆

FORMAT READ: EBOOK / PRINT / AUDIOBOOK

131

✓ **SYNOPSIS/THINGS I LIKED:**

_____

_____

_____

_____

🚫 **THINGS I DIDN'T LIKE:**

_____

_____

_____

_____

✏️ **FAVORITE QUOTE(S):**

_____

_____

_____

_____

_____

_____

_____

TITLE: _____

GENRE: _____

SERIES: _____

AUTHOR: _____

PAGES: _____

STARTED: _____

FINISHED: _____

☆ ☆ ☆ ☆ ☆

FORMAT READ: EBOOK / PRINT / AUDIOBOOK

TITLE: _____

GENRE: _____

SERIES: _____

AUTHOR: _____

PAGES: _____

STARTED: _____

FINISHED: _____

☆ ☆ ☆ ☆ ☆

FORMAT READ: EBOOK / PRINT / AUDIOBOOK

☑ **SYNOPSIS/THINGS I LIKED:**

_____
_____
_____
_____

🚫 **THINGS I DIDN'T LIKE:**

_____
_____
_____
_____

✒ **FAVORITE QUOTE(S):**

_____
_____
_____
_____
_____
_____

TITLE: _____

GENRE: _____

SERIES: _____

AUTHOR: _____

PAGES: _____

STARTED: _____

FINISHED: _____

☆ ☆ ☆ ☆ ☆

FORMAT READ: EBOOK / PRINT / AUDIOBOOK

✓ **SYNOPSIS/THINGS I LIKED:**

_____
_____
_____
_____

🚫 **THINGS I DIDN'T LIKE:**

_____
_____
_____
_____

✒ **FAVORITE QUOTE(S):**

_____
_____
_____
_____
_____
_____
_____

✓ SYNOPSIS/THINGS I LIKED:

_____
_____
_____
_____

🚫 THINGS I DIDN'T LIKE:

_____
_____
_____
_____

✏️ FAVORITE QUOTE(S):

_____
_____
_____
_____
_____
_____
_____

TITLE: _____

GENRE: _____

SERIES: _____

AUTHOR: _____

PAGES: _____

STARTED: _____

FINISHED: _____

☆☆☆☆☆

FORMAT READ: EBOOK / PRINT / AUDIOBOOK

135

✓ **SYNOPSIS/THINGS I LIKED:**

_____
_____
_____
_____
_____

🚫 **THINGS I DIDN'T LIKE:**

_____
_____
_____
_____

✏️ **FAVORITE QUOTE(S):**

_____
_____
_____
_____
_____
_____
_____

TITLE: _____

GENRE: _____

SERIES: _____

AUTHOR: _____

PAGES: _____

STARTED: _____

FINISHED: _____

☆ ☆ ☆ ☆ ☆

FORMAT READ: EBOOK / PRINT / AUDIOBOOK

TITLE: _____

GENRE: _____

SERIES: _____

AUTHOR: _____

PAGES: _____

STARTED: _____

FINISHED: _____

☆ ☆ ☆ ☆ ☆

FORMAT READ: EBOOK / PRINT / AUDIOBOOK

☑ **SYNOPSIS/THINGS I LIKED:**

_____
_____
_____
_____
_____

🚫 **THINGS I DIDN'T LIKE:**

_____
_____
_____
_____

📝 **FAVORITE QUOTE(S):**

_____
_____
_____
_____
_____
_____
_____
_____

TITLE: _____

GENRE: _____

SERIES: _____

AUTHOR: _____

PAGES: _____

STARTED: _____

FINISHED: _____

☆☆☆☆☆

FORMAT READ: EBOOK / PRINT / AUDIOBOOK

✅ **SYNOPSIS/THINGS I LIKED:**

_____

_____

_____

_____

🚫 **THINGS I DIDN'T LIKE:**

_____

_____

_____

_____

✎ **FAVORITE QUOTE(S):**

_____

_____

_____

_____

_____

_____

✓ SYNOPSIS/THINGS I LIKED:

_____

_____

_____

_____

🚫 THINGS I DIDN'T LIKE:

_____

_____

_____

_____

📝 FAVORITE QUOTE(S):

_____

_____

_____

_____

_____

_____

TITLE: _____

GENRE: _____

SERIES: _____

AUTHOR: _____

PAGES: _____

STARTED: _____

FINISHED: _____

☆ ☆ ☆ ☆ ☆

FORMAT READ: EBOOK / PRINT / AUDIOBOOK

139

✓ SYNOPSIS/THINGS I LIKED:

_____
_____
_____
_____

🚫 THINGS I DIDN'T LIKE:

_____
_____
_____
_____

✏️ FAVORITE QUOTE(S):

_____
_____
_____
_____
_____
_____

TITLE: _____

GENRE: _____

SERIES: _____

AUTHOR: _____

PAGES: _____

STARTED: _____

FINISHED: _____

☆ ☆ ☆ ☆ ☆

FORMAT READ: EBOOK / PRINT / AUDIOBOOK

TITLE: _____

GENRE: _____

SERIES: _____

AUTHOR: _____

PAGES: _____

STARTED: _____

FINISHED: _____

☆☆☆☆☆

FORMAT READ: EBOOK / PRINT / AUDIOBOOK

✔ SYNOPSIS/THINGS I LIKED:

_____
_____
_____
_____
_____

🚫 THINGS I DIDN'T LIKE:

_____
_____
_____
_____

✎ FAVORITE QUOTE(S):

_____
_____
_____
_____
_____
_____
_____

TITLE: _____

GENRE: _____

SERIES: _____

AUTHOR: _____

PAGES: _____

STARTED: _____

FINISHED: _____

☆ ☆ ☆ ☆ ☆

FORMAT READ: EBOOK / PRINT / AUDIOBOOK

✓ **SYNOPSIS/THINGS I LIKED:**

_____
_____
_____
_____

🚫 **THINGS I DIDN'T LIKE:**

_____
_____
_____
_____

✍ **FAVORITE QUOTE(S):**

_____
_____
_____
_____
_____
_____
_____

✅ SYNOPSIS/THINGS I LIKED:

_____
_____
_____
_____

🚫 THINGS I DIDN'T LIKE:

_____
_____
_____
_____

📝 FAVORITE QUOTE(S):

_____
_____
_____
_____
_____
_____

TITLE: _____

GENRE: _____

SERIES: _____

AUTHOR: _____

PAGES: _____

STARTED: _____

FINISHED: _____

☆ ☆ ☆ ☆ ☆

FORMAT READ: EBOOK / PRINT / AUDIOBOOK

☑ **SYNOPSIS/THINGS I LIKED:**

_____
_____
_____
_____
_____

🚫 **THINGS I DIDN'T LIKE:**

_____
_____
_____
_____

✏️ **FAVORITE QUOTE(S):**

_____
_____
_____
_____
_____
_____
_____

TITLE: _____

GENRE: _____

SERIES: _____

AUTHOR: _____

PAGES: _____

STARTED: _____

FINISHED: _____

☆ ☆ ☆ ☆ ☆

FORMAT READ: EBOOK / PRINT / AUDIOBOOK

TITLE: _____

GENRE: _____

SERIES: _____

AUTHOR: _____

PAGES: _____

STARTED: _____

FINISHED: _____

☆☆☆☆☆

FORMAT READ: EBOOK / PRINT / AUDIOBOOK

☑ SYNOPSIS/THINGS I LIKED:

_____

_____

_____

_____

🚫 THINGS I DIDN'T LIKE:

_____

_____

_____

_____

✎ FAVORITE QUOTE(S):

_____

_____

_____

_____

_____

_____

_____

TITLE: _____

GENRE: _____

SERIES: _____

AUTHOR: _____

PAGES: _____

STARTED: _____

FINISHED: _____

☆ ☆ ☆ ☆ ☆

FORMAT READ: EBOOK / PRINT / AUDIOBOOK

☑ **SYNOPSIS/THINGS I LIKED:**

_____
_____
_____
_____

🚫 **THINGS I DIDN'T LIKE:**

_____
_____
_____
_____

✎ **FAVORITE QUOTE(S):**

_____
_____
_____
_____
_____
_____

✓ **Synopsis/Things I liked:**

_____
_____
_____
_____
_____

🚫 **Things I didn't like:**

_____
_____
_____
_____

✎ **Favorite quote(s):**

_____
_____
_____
_____
_____
_____
_____

Title: _____

Genre: _____

Series: _____

Author: _____

Pages: _____

Started: _____

Finished: _____

☆ ☆ ☆ ☆ ☆

Format read: Ebook / Print / Audiobook

_____

_____

_____

_____

_____

🚫 THINGS I DIDN'T LIKE:

_____

_____

_____

_____

✎ FAVORITE QUOTE(S):

_____

_____

_____

_____

_____

_____

TITLE: _____

GENRE: _____

SERIES: _____

AUTHOR: _____

PAGES: _____

STARTED: _____

FINISHED: _____

☆ ☆ ☆ ☆ ☆

FORMAT READ: EBOOK / PRINT / AUDIOBOOK

TITLE: _____

GENRE: _____

SERIES: _____

AUTHOR: _____

PAGES: _____

STARTED: _____

FINISHED: _____

☆ ☆ ☆ ☆ ☆

FORMAT READ: EBOOK / PRINT / AUDIOBOOK

✔ SYNOPSIS/THINGS I LIKED:

_____

_____

_____

_____

🚫 THINGS I DIDN'T LIKE:

_____

_____

_____

_____

✎ FAVORITE QUOTE(S):

_____

_____

_____

_____

_____

_____

_____

TITLE: _____

GENRE: _____

SERIES: _____

AUTHOR: _____

PAGES: _____

STARTED: _____

FINISHED: _____

☆☆☆☆☆

FORMAT READ: EBOOK / PRINT / AUDIOBOOK

✅ **SYNOPSIS/THINGS I LIKED:**

_____
_____
_____
_____

🚫 **THINGS I DIDN'T LIKE:**

_____
_____
_____
_____

✏️ **FAVORITE QUOTE(S):**

_____
_____
_____
_____
_____
_____
_____

✓ **SYNOPSIS/THINGS I LIKED:**

_____

_____

_____

_____

_____

🚫 **THINGS I DIDN'T LIKE:**

_____

_____

_____

_____

✎ **FAVORITE QUOTE(S):**

_____

_____

_____

_____

_____

_____

TITLE: _____

GENRE: _____

SERIES: _____

AUTHOR: _____

PAGES: _____

STARTED: _____

FINISHED: _____

☆ ☆ ☆ ☆ ☆

FORMAT READ: EBOOK / PRINT / AUDIOBOOK

151

✔️ **SYNOPSIS/THINGS I LIKED:**

_____
_____
_____
_____

🚫 **THINGS I DIDN'T LIKE:**

_____
_____
_____
_____

✏️ **FAVORITE QUOTE(S):**

_____
_____
_____
_____
_____
_____

TITLE: _____

GENRE: _____

SERIES: _____

AUTHOR: _____

PAGES: _____

STARTED: _____

FINISHED: _____

☆ ☆ ☆ ☆ ☆

FORMAT READ: EBOOK / PRINT / AUDIOBOOK

TITLE: _____

GENRE: _____

SERIES: _____

AUTHOR: _____

PAGES: _____

STARTED: _____

FINISHED: _____

☆☆☆☆☆

FORMAT READ: EBOOK / PRINT / AUDIOBOOK

✓ **SYNOPSIS/THINGS I LIKED:** _____
_____
_____
_____

🚫 **THINGS I DIDN'T LIKE:** _____
_____
_____
_____

📝 **FAVORITE QUOTE(S):** _____
_____
_____
_____
_____
_____
_____

TITLE: _____

GENRE: _____

SERIES: _____

AUTHOR: _____

PAGES: _____

STARTED: _____

FINISHED: _____

☆☆☆☆☆

FORMAT READ: EBOOK / PRINT / AUDIOBOOK

✔ **SYNOPSIS/THINGS I LIKED:**

_____
_____
_____
_____

🚫 **THINGS I DIDN'T LIKE:**

_____
_____
_____
_____

✎ **FAVORITE QUOTE(S):**

_____
_____
_____
_____
_____
_____
_____

✔ **Synopsis/Things I liked:**

_____

_____

_____

_____

_____

🚫 **Things I didn't like:**

_____

_____

_____

_____

_____

✎ **Favorite quote(s):**

_____

_____

_____

_____

_____

_____

_____

Title: _____

Genre: _____

Series: _____

Author: _____

Pages: _____

Started: _____

Finished: _____

☆ ☆ ☆ ☆ ☆

Format read: Ebook / Print / Audiobook

✔ SYNOPSIS/THINGS I LIKED:

✔ SYNOPSIS/THINGS I LIKED:

_____

_____

_____

_____

🚫 THINGS I DIDN'T LIKE:

_____

_____

_____

_____

✎ FAVORITE QUOTE(S):

_____

_____

_____

_____

_____

_____

TITLE: _____

GENRE: _____

SERIES: _____

AUTHOR: _____

PAGES: _____

STARTED: _____

FINISHED: _____

☆ ☆ ☆ ☆ ☆

FORMAT READ: EBOOK / PRINT / AUDIOBOOK

TITLE: _____

GENRE: _____

SERIES: _____

AUTHOR: _____

PAGES: _____

STARTED: _____

FINISHED: _____

☆☆☆☆☆

FORMAT READ: EBOOK / PRINT / AUDIOBOOK

✔ **SYNOPSIS/THINGS I LIKED:**

_____
_____
_____
_____

🚫 **THINGS I DIDN'T LIKE:**

_____
_____
_____
_____

📝 **FAVORITE QUOTE(S):**

_____
_____
_____
_____
_____
_____

TITLE: _____

GENRE: _____

SERIES: _____

AUTHOR: _____

PAGES: _____

STARTED: _____

FINISHED: _____

☆ ☆ ☆ ☆ ☆

FORMAT READ: EBOOK / PRINT / AUDIOBOOK

✓ **SYNOPSIS/THINGS I LIKED:**

_____
_____
_____
_____

🚫 **THINGS I DIDN'T LIKE:**

_____
_____
_____

✎ **FAVORITE QUOTE(S):**

_____
_____
_____
_____
_____
_____

✓ **SYNOPSIS/THINGS I LIKED:**

_____

_____

_____

_____

_____

🚫 **THINGS I DIDN'T LIKE:**

_____

_____

_____

_____

✏️ **FAVORITE QUOTE(S):**

_____

_____

_____

_____

_____

_____

_____

TITLE: _____

GENRE: _____

SERIES: _____

AUTHOR: _____

PAGES: _____

STARTED: _____

FINISHED: _____

☆ ☆ ☆ ☆ ☆

FORMAT READ: EBOOK / PRINT / AUDIOBOOK

159

✓ **SYNOPSIS/THINGS I LIKED:**

_____

_____

_____

_____

🚫 **THINGS I DIDN'T LIKE:**

_____

_____

_____

_____

✎ **FAVORITE QUOTE(S):**

_____

_____

_____

_____

_____

TITLE: _____

GENRE: _____

SERIES: _____

AUTHOR: _____

PAGES: _____

STARTED: _____

FINISHED: _____

☆ ☆ ☆ ☆ ☆

FORMAT READ: EBOOK / PRINT / AUDIOBOOK

TITLE: _____

GENRE: _____

SERIES: _____

AUTHOR: _____

PAGES: _____

STARTED: _____

FINISHED: _____

☆ ☆ ☆ ☆ ☆

FORMAT READ: EBOOK / PRINT / AUDIOBOOK

✓ **SYNOPSIS/THINGS I LIKED:**

_____
_____
_____
_____

🚫 **THINGS I DIDN'T LIKE:**

_____
_____
_____
_____

✏️ **FAVORITE QUOTE(S):**

_____
_____
_____
_____
_____
_____
_____

TITLE: _____

GENRE: _____

SERIES: _____

AUTHOR: _____

PAGES: _____

STARTED: _____

FINISHED: _____

☆ ☆ ☆ ☆ ☆

FORMAT READ: EBOOK / PRINT / AUDIOBOOK

✓ **SYNOPSIS/THINGS I LIKED:**

_____
_____
_____
_____

🚫 **THINGS I DIDN'T LIKE:**

_____
_____
_____

✏️ **FAVORITE QUOTE(S):**

_____
_____
_____
_____
_____
_____
_____

☑ **SYNOPSIS/THINGS I LIKED:**

_____

_____

_____

_____

🚫 **THINGS I DIDN'T LIKE:**

_____

_____

_____

_____

📝 **FAVORITE QUOTE(S):**

_____

_____

_____

_____

_____

_____

TITLE: _____

GENRE: _____

SERIES: _____

AUTHOR: _____

PAGES: _____

STARTED: _____

FINISHED: _____

☆ ☆ ☆ ☆ ☆

FORMAT READ: EBOOK / PRINT / AUDIOBOOK

163

✔ Synopsis/Things I liked:

_____

_____

_____

_____

_____

🚫 Things I didn't like:

_____

_____

_____

_____

✎ Favorite quote(s):

_____

_____

_____

_____

_____

_____

_____

Title: _____

Genre: _____

Series: _____

Author: _____

Pages: _____

Started: _____

Finished: _____

☆ ☆ ☆ ☆ ☆

Format read: Ebook / Print / Audiobook

TITLE: _____

GENRE: _____

SERIES: _____

AUTHOR: _____

PAGES: _____

STARTED: _____

FINISHED: _____

☆☆☆☆☆

FORMAT READ: EBOOK / PRINT / AUDIOBOOK

✓ SYNOPSIS/THINGS I LIKED:

_____

_____

_____

_____

🚫 THINGS I DIDN'T LIKE:

_____

_____

_____

_____

✏ FAVORITE QUOTE(S):

_____

_____

_____

_____

_____

_____

_____

TITLE: _____

GENRE: _____

SERIES: _____

AUTHOR: _____

PAGES: _____

STARTED: _____

FINISHED: _____

☆ ☆ ☆ ☆ ☆

FORMAT READ: EBOOK / PRINT / AUDIOBOOK

✓ **SYNOPSIS/THINGS I LIKED:**

_____
_____
_____
_____

🚫 **THINGS I DIDN'T LIKE:**

_____
_____
_____

✒ **FAVORITE QUOTE(S):**

_____
_____
_____
_____
_____
_____

✓ **SYNOPSIS/THINGS I LIKED:**

_____
_____
_____
_____

🚫 **THINGS I DIDN'T LIKE:**

_____
_____
_____
_____

✎ **FAVORITE QUOTE(S):**

_____
_____
_____
_____
_____
_____

TITLE: _____

GENRE: _____

SERIES: _____

AUTHOR: _____

PAGES: _____

STARTED: _____

FINISHED: _____

☆ ☆ ☆ ☆ ☆

FORMAT READ: EBOOK / PRINT / AUDIOBOOK

✓ **SYNOPSIS/THINGS I LIKED:**

_____

_____

_____

_____

🚫 **THINGS I DIDN'T LIKE:**

_____

_____

_____

_____

✏️ **FAVORITE QUOTE(S):**

_____

_____

_____

_____

_____

_____

TITLE: _____

GENRE: _____

SERIES: _____

AUTHOR: _____

PAGES: _____

STARTED: _____

FINISHED: _____

☆ ☆ ☆ ☆ ☆

FORMAT READ: EBOOK / PRINT / AUDIOBOOK

TITLE: _____

GENRE: _____

SERIES: _____

AUTHOR: _____

PAGES: _____

STARTED: _____

FINISHED: _____

☆ ☆ ☆ ☆ ☆

FORMAT READ: EBOOK / PRINT / AUDIOBOOK

✔ SYNOPSIS/THINGS I LIKED: _____

_____

_____

_____

_____

🚫 THINGS I DIDN'T LIKE: _____

_____

_____

_____

✏ FAVORITE QUOTE(S): _____

_____

_____

_____

_____

_____

_____

169

TITLE: _____

GENRE: _____

SERIES: _____

AUTHOR: _____

PAGES: _____

STARTED: _____

FINISHED: _____

☆ ☆ ☆ ☆ ☆

FORMAT READ: EBOOK / PRINT / AUDIOBOOK

✓ **SYNOPSIS/THINGS I LIKED:**

_____
_____
_____
_____

🚫 **THINGS I DIDN'T LIKE:**

_____
_____
_____
_____

✎ **FAVORITE QUOTE(S):**

_____
_____
_____
_____
_____
_____
_____

✅ **SYNOPSIS/THINGS I LIKED:**

_____
_____
_____
_____
_____

🚫 **THINGS I DIDN'T LIKE:**

_____
_____
_____
_____

✏️ **FAVORITE QUOTE(S):**

_____
_____
_____
_____
_____
_____
_____

TITLE: _____

GENRE: _____

SERIES: _____

AUTHOR: _____

PAGES: _____

STARTED: _____

FINISHED: _____

☆ ☆ ☆ ☆ ☆

FORMAT READ: EBOOK / PRINT / AUDIOBOOK

✔ SYNOPSIS/THINGS I LIKED:

_____

_____

_____

_____

🚫 THINGS I DIDN'T LIKE:

_____

_____

_____

_____

✏ FAVORITE QUOTE(S):

_____

_____

_____

_____

_____

_____

_____

TITLE: _____

GENRE: _____

SERIES: _____

AUTHOR: _____

PAGES: _____

STARTED: _____

FINISHED: _____

☆ ☆ ☆ ☆ ☆

FORMAT READ: EBOOK / PRINT / AUDIOBOOK

TITLE: _____

GENRE: _____

SERIES: _____

AUTHOR: _____

PAGES: _____

STARTED: _____

FINISHED: _____

☆☆☆☆☆

FORMAT READ: EBOOK / PRINT / AUDIOBOOK

✓ **SYNOPSIS/THINGS I LIKED:**

_____
_____
_____
_____
_____

🚫 **THINGS I DIDN'T LIKE:**

_____
_____
_____
_____

✏️ **FAVORITE QUOTE(S):**

_____
_____
_____
_____
_____
_____
_____

TITLE: _____

GENRE: _____

SERIES: _____

AUTHOR: _____

PAGES: _____

STARTED: _____

FINISHED: _____

☆ ☆ ☆ ☆ ☆

FORMAT READ: EBOOK / PRINT / AUDIOBOOK

✓ **SYNOPSIS/THINGS I LIKED:**

_____
_____
_____
_____
_____

🚫 **THINGS I DIDN'T LIKE:**

_____
_____
_____
_____

✏️ **FAVORITE QUOTE(S):**

_____
_____
_____
_____
_____
_____
_____
_____

✓ **SYNOPSIS/THINGS I LIKED:**

_____
_____
_____
_____
_____

🚫 **THINGS I DIDN'T LIKE:**

_____
_____
_____
_____

✏️ **FAVORITE QUOTE(S):**

_____
_____
_____
_____
_____
_____
_____

TITLE: _____

GENRE: _____

SERIES: _____

AUTHOR: _____

PAGES: _____

STARTED: _____

FINISHED: _____

☆ ☆ ☆ ☆ ☆

FORMAT READ: EBOOK / PRINT / AUDIOBOOK

✔ **SYNOPSIS/THINGS I LIKED:**

_____
_____
_____
_____

🚫 **THINGS I DIDN'T LIKE:**

_____
_____
_____
_____

✏️ **FAVORITE QUOTE(S):**

_____
_____
_____
_____
_____
_____
_____

TITLE: _____

GENRE: _____

SERIES: _____

AUTHOR: _____

PAGES: _____

STARTED: _____

FINISHED: _____

☆ ☆ ☆ ☆ ☆

FORMAT READ: EBOOK / PRINT / AUDIOBOOK

TITLE: _____

GENRE: _____

SERIES: _____

AUTHOR: _____

PAGES: _____

STARTED: _____

FINISHED: _____

☆☆☆☆☆

FORMAT READ: EBOOK / PRINT / AUDIOBOOK

✓ SYNOPSIS/THINGS I LIKED: _____
_____
_____
_____

🚫 THINGS I DIDN'T LIKE: _____
_____
_____
_____

✐ FAVORITE QUOTE(S): _____
_____
_____
_____
_____
_____
_____

TITLE: _____

GENRE: _____

SERIES: _____

AUTHOR: _____

PAGES: _____

STARTED: _____

FINISHED: _____

☆ ☆ ☆ ☆ ☆

FORMAT READ: EBOOK / PRINT / AUDIOBOOK

✓ **SYNOPSIS/THINGS I LIKED:**

_____
_____
_____
_____

🚫 **THINGS I DIDN'T LIKE:**

_____
_____
_____
_____

✎ **FAVORITE QUOTE(S):**

_____
_____
_____
_____
_____
_____
_____

✓ **SYNOPSIS/THINGS I LIKED:**

_____
_____
_____
_____

🚫 **THINGS I DIDN'T LIKE:**

_____
_____
_____
_____

✎ **FAVORITE QUOTE(S):**

_____
_____
_____
_____
_____
_____

TITLE: _____

GENRE: _____

SERIES: _____

AUTHOR: _____

PAGES: _____

STARTED: _____

FINISHED: _____

☆ ☆ ☆ ☆ ☆

FORMAT READ: EBOOK / PRINT / AUDIOBOOK

✓ **SYNOPSIS/THINGS I LIKED:**

_____

_____

_____

_____

_____

🚫 **THINGS I DIDN'T LIKE:**

_____

_____

_____

_____

_____

✎ **FAVORITE QUOTE(S):**

_____

_____

_____

_____

_____

_____

_____

TITLE: _____

GENRE: _____

SERIES: _____

AUTHOR: _____

PAGES: _____

STARTED: _____

FINISHED: _____

☆ ☆ ☆ ☆ ☆

FORMAT READ: EBOOK / PRINT / AUDIOBOOK

TITLE: _____

GENRE: _____

SERIES: _____

AUTHOR: _____

PAGES: _____

STARTED: _____

FINISHED: _____

☆☆☆☆☆

FORMAT READ: EBOOK / PRINT / AUDIOBOOK

✔ SYNOPSIS/THINGS I LIKED:

_____
_____
_____
_____

🚫 THINGS I DIDN'T LIKE:

_____
_____
_____
_____

✎ FAVORITE QUOTE(S):

_____
_____
_____
_____
_____
_____

TITLE: _____

GENRE: _____

SERIES: _____

AUTHOR: _____

PAGES: _____

STARTED: _____

FINISHED: _____

☆ ☆ ☆ ☆ ☆

FORMAT READ: EBOOK / PRINT / AUDIOBOOK

☑ **SYNOPSIS/THINGS I LIKED:**

_____

_____

_____

_____

_____

🚫 **THINGS I DIDN'T LIKE:**

_____

_____

_____

_____

✏️ **FAVORITE QUOTE(S):**

_____

_____

_____

_____

_____

_____

☑ **Synopsis/Things I liked:**

_____
_____
_____
_____
_____

🚫 **Things I didn't like:**

_____
_____
_____
_____

📝 **Favorite quote(s):**

_____
_____
_____
_____
_____
_____
_____

Title: _____

Genre: _____

Series: _____

Author: _____

Pages: _____

Started: _____

Finished: _____

☆☆☆☆☆

Format read: Ebook / Print / Audiobook

☑ **SYNOPSIS/THINGS I LIKED:**

_____

_____

_____

_____

🚫 **THINGS I DIDN'T LIKE:**

_____

_____

_____

_____

📝 **FAVORITE QUOTE(S):**

_____

_____

_____

_____

_____

_____

TITLE: _____

GENRE: _____

SERIES: _____

AUTHOR: _____

PAGES: _____

STARTED: _____

FINISHED: _____

☆ ☆ ☆ ☆ ☆

FORMAT READ: EBOOK / PRINT / AUDIOBOOK

TITLE: _____

GENRE: _____

SERIES: _____

AUTHOR: _____

PAGES: _____

STARTED: _____

FINISHED: _____

☆ ☆ ☆ ☆ ☆

FORMAT READ: EBOOK / PRINT / AUDIOBOOK

✔ SYNOPSIS/THINGS I LIKED:
_____
_____
_____
_____

🚫 THINGS I DIDN'T LIKE:
_____
_____
_____
_____

✎ FAVORITE QUOTE(S):
_____
_____
_____
_____
_____
_____

TITLE: _____

GENRE: _____

SERIES: _____

AUTHOR: _____

PAGES: _____

STARTED: _____

FINISHED: _____

☆☆☆☆☆

FORMAT READ: EBOOK / PRINT / AUDIOBOOK

✓ **SYNOPSIS/THINGS I LIKED:**

_____
_____
_____
_____

🚫 **THINGS I DIDN'T LIKE:**

_____
_____
_____
_____

📝 **FAVORITE QUOTE(S):**

_____
_____
_____
_____
_____
_____
_____

✓ **Synopsis/Things I liked:**

_____

_____

_____

_____

🚫 **Things I didn't like:**

_____

_____

_____

_____

✎ **Favorite quote(s):**

_____

_____

_____

_____

_____

_____

Title: _____

Genre: _____

Series: _____

Author: _____

Pages: _____

Started: _____

Finished: _____

☆ ☆ ☆ ☆ ☆

Format read: Ebook / Print / Audiobook

✔ **Synopsis/Things I liked:**

_____

_____

_____

_____

🚫 **Things I didn't like:**

_____

_____

_____

_____

✎ **Favorite quote(s):**

_____

_____

_____

_____

_____

_____

Title: _____

Genre: _____

Series: _____

Author: _____

Pages: _____

Started: _____

Finished: _____

☆ ☆ ☆ ☆ ☆

Format read: Ebook / Print / Audiobook

TITLE: _____

GENRE: _____

SERIES: _____

AUTHOR: _____

PAGES: _____

STARTED: _____

FINISHED: _____

☆☆☆☆☆

FORMAT READ: EBOOK / PRINT / AUDIOBOOK

✓ SYNOPSIS/THINGS I LIKED:

_____
_____
_____
_____

🚫 THINGS I DIDN'T LIKE:

_____
_____
_____
_____

✎ FAVORITE QUOTE(S):

_____
_____
_____
_____
_____
_____
_____

TITLE: _____

GENRE: _____

SERIES: _____

AUTHOR: _____

PAGES: _____

STARTED: _____

FINISHED: _____

☆☆☆☆☆

FORMAT READ: EBOOK / PRINT / AUDIOBOOK

☑ **SYNOPSIS/THINGS I LIKED:**

_____
_____
_____
_____

🚫 **THINGS I DIDN'T LIKE:**

_____
_____
_____
_____

📝 **FAVORITE QUOTE(S):**

_____
_____
_____
_____
_____
_____

✔ **SYNOPSIS/THINGS I LIKED:**

_____
_____
_____
_____

🚫 **THINGS I DIDN'T LIKE:**

_____
_____
_____
_____

📝 **FAVORITE QUOTE(S):**

_____
_____
_____
_____
_____
_____

TITLE: _____

GENRE: _____

SERIES: _____

AUTHOR: _____

PAGES: _____

STARTED: _____

FINISHED: _____

☆ ☆ ☆ ☆ ☆

FORMAT READ: EBOOK / PRINT / AUDIOBOOK

✓ **Synopsis/Things I liked:**

_____
_____
_____
_____
_____

🚫 **Things I didn't like:**

_____
_____
_____
_____
_____

✏️ **Favorite quote(s):**

_____
_____
_____
_____
_____
_____
_____

Title: _____

Genre: _____

Series: _____

Author: _____

Pages: _____

Started: _____

Finished: _____

☆ ☆ ☆ ☆ ☆

Format read: Ebook / Print / Audiobook

TITLE: _____

GENRE: _____

SERIES: _____

AUTHOR: _____

PAGES: _____

STARTED: _____

FINISHED: _____

☆ ☆ ☆ ☆ ☆

FORMAT READ: EBOOK / PRINT / AUDIOBOOK

SYNOPSIS/THINGS I LIKED:

_____

_____

_____

_____

THINGS I DIDN'T LIKE:

_____

_____

_____

_____

FAVORITE QUOTE(S):

_____

_____

_____

_____

_____

_____

_____

TITLE: _____

GENRE: _____

SERIES: _____

AUTHOR: _____

PAGES: _____

STARTED: _____

FINISHED: _____

☆ ☆ ☆ ☆ ☆

FORMAT READ: EBOOK / PRINT / AUDIOBOOK

✓ **SYNOPSIS/THINGS I LIKED:**

_____
_____
_____
_____

🚫 **THINGS I DIDN'T LIKE:**

_____
_____
_____
_____

📝 **FAVORITE QUOTE(S):**

_____
_____
_____
_____
_____
_____
_____

✓ SYNOPSIS/THINGS I LIKED:

_____
_____
_____
_____

🚫 THINGS I DIDN'T LIKE:

_____
_____
_____
_____

✏️ FAVORITE QUOTE(S):

_____
_____
_____
_____
_____
_____

TITLE: _____

GENRE: _____

SERIES: _____

AUTHOR: _____

PAGES: _____

STARTED: _____

FINISHED: _____

☆ ☆ ☆ ☆ ☆

FORMAT READ: EBOOK / PRINT / AUDIOBOOK

✔ SYNOPSIS/THINGS I LIKED:

_____
_____
_____
_____

🚫 THINGS I DIDN'T LIKE:

_____
_____
_____
_____

✎ FAVORITE QUOTE(S):

_____
_____
_____
_____
_____
_____

TITLE: _____

GENRE: _____

SERIES: _____

AUTHOR: _____

PAGES: _____

STARTED: _____

FINISHED: _____

☆ ☆ ☆ ☆ ☆

FORMAT READ: EBOOK / PRINT / AUDIOBOOK

TITLE: _____

GENRE: _____

SERIES: _____

AUTHOR: _____

PAGES: _____

STARTED: _____

FINISHED: _____

☆ ☆ ☆ ☆ ☆

FORMAT READ: EBOOK / PRINT / AUDIOBOOK

✓ SYNOPSIS/THINGS I LIKED:

_____

_____

_____

_____

⊘ THINGS I DIDN'T LIKE:

_____

_____

_____

_____

✐ FAVORITE QUOTE(S):

_____

_____

_____

_____

_____

_____

_____

TITLE: _____

GENRE: _____

SERIES: _____

AUTHOR: _____

PAGES: _____

STARTED: _____

FINISHED: _____

☆☆☆☆☆

FORMAT READ: EBOOK / PRINT / AUDIOBOOK

✓ **SYNOPSIS/THINGS I LIKED:**

_____
_____
_____
_____

🚫 **THINGS I DIDN'T LIKE:**

_____
_____
_____
_____

✎ **FAVORITE QUOTE(S):**

_____
_____
_____
_____
_____
_____
_____

198

✔ SYNOPSIS/THINGS I LIKED:

_____

_____

_____

_____

🚫 THINGS I DIDN'T LIKE:

_____

_____

_____

_____

✎ FAVORITE QUOTE(S):

_____

_____

_____

_____

_____

_____

TITLE: _____

GENRE: _____

SERIES: _____

AUTHOR: _____

PAGES: _____

STARTED: _____

FINISHED: _____

☆ ☆ ☆ ☆ ☆

FORMAT READ: EBOOK / PRINT / AUDIOBOOK

199

✓ **SYNOPSIS/THINGS I LIKED:**

_____

_____

_____

_____

🚫 **THINGS I DIDN'T LIKE:**

_____

_____

_____

_____

📝 **FAVORITE QUOTE(S):**

_____

_____

_____

_____

_____

_____

TITLE: _____

GENRE: _____

SERIES: _____

AUTHOR: _____

PAGES: _____

STARTED: _____

FINISHED: _____

☆ ☆ ☆ ☆ ☆

FORMAT READ: EBOOK / PRINT / AUDIOBOOK

TITLE: _____

GENRE: _____

SERIES: _____

AUTHOR: _____

PAGES: _____

STARTED: _____

FINISHED: _____

☆☆☆☆☆

FORMAT READ: EBOOK / PRINT / AUDIOBOOK

✓ **SYNOPSIS/THINGS I LIKED:** _____

_____
_____
_____

🚫 **THINGS I DIDN'T LIKE:** _____

_____
_____
_____

📝 **FAVORITE QUOTE(S):** _____

_____
_____
_____
_____
_____
_____

TITLE: _____

GENRE: _____

SERIES: _____

AUTHOR: _____

PAGES: _____

STARTED: _____

FINISHED: _____

☆ ☆ ☆ ☆ ☆

FORMAT READ: EBOOK / PRINT / AUDIOBOOK

✓ **SYNOPSIS/THINGS I LIKED:**

_____
_____
_____
_____

🚫 **THINGS I DIDN'T LIKE:**

_____
_____
_____
_____

✎ **FAVORITE QUOTE(S):**

_____
_____
_____
_____
_____
_____

✓ **SYNOPSIS/THINGS I LIKED:**

_____
_____
_____
_____

🚫 **THINGS I DIDN'T LIKE:**

_____
_____
_____
_____

✎ **FAVORITE QUOTE(S):**

_____
_____
_____
_____
_____
_____

TITLE: _____

GENRE: _____

SERIES: _____

AUTHOR: _____

PAGES: _____

STARTED: _____

FINISHED: _____

☆ ☆ ☆ ☆ ☆

FORMAT READ: EBOOK / PRINT / AUDIOBOOK

✔ **SYNOPSIS/THINGS I LIKED:**

_____

_____

_____

_____

🚫 **THINGS I DIDN'T LIKE:**

_____

_____

_____

_____

✎ **FAVORITE QUOTE(S):**

_____

_____

_____

_____

_____

_____

_____

TITLE: _____

GENRE: _____

SERIES: _____

AUTHOR: _____

PAGES: _____

STARTED: _____

FINISHED: _____

☆ ☆ ☆ ☆ ☆

FORMAT READ: EBOOK / PRINT / AUDIOBOOK

TITLE: _____

GENRE: _____

SERIES: _____

AUTHOR: _____

PAGES: _____

STARTED: _____

FINISHED: _____

☆☆☆☆☆

FORMAT READ: EBOOK / PRINT / AUDIOBOOK

✓ SYNOPSIS/THINGS I LIKED:

_____
_____
_____
_____

🚫 THINGS I DIDN'T LIKE:

_____
_____
_____
_____

✍ FAVORITE QUOTE(S):

_____
_____
_____
_____
_____
_____
_____

TITLE: _____

GENRE: _____

SERIES: _____

AUTHOR: _____

PAGES: _____

STARTED: _____

FINISHED: _____

☆ ☆ ☆ ☆ ☆

FORMAT READ: EBOOK / PRINT / AUDIOBOOK

✓ **SYNOPSIS/THINGS I LIKED:**

_____
_____
_____
_____
_____

🚫 **THINGS I DIDN'T LIKE:**

_____
_____
_____
_____

✎ **FAVORITE QUOTE(S):**

_____
_____
_____
_____
_____
_____

✔ SYNOPSIS/THINGS I LIKED:
_____
_____
_____
_____
_____

🚫 THINGS I DIDN'T LIKE:
_____
_____
_____
_____

✎ FAVORITE QUOTE(S):
_____
_____
_____
_____
_____
_____
_____

TITLE: _____

GENRE: _____

SERIES: _____

AUTHOR: _____

PAGES: _____

STARTED: _____

FINISHED: _____

☆ ☆ ☆ ☆ ☆

FORMAT READ: EBOOK / PRINT / AUDIOBOOK

207

✓ SYNOPSIS/THINGS I LIKED:

_____
_____
_____
_____

🚫 THINGS I DIDN'T LIKE:

_____
_____
_____
_____

✎ FAVORITE QUOTE(S):

_____
_____
_____
_____
_____
_____

TITLE: _____

GENRE: _____

SERIES: _____

AUTHOR: _____

PAGES: _____

STARTED: _____

FINISHED: _____

☆ ☆ ☆ ☆ ☆

FORMAT READ: EBOOK / PRINT / AUDIOBOOK

TITLE: _____

GENRE: _____

SERIES: _____

AUTHOR: _____

PAGES: _____

STARTED: _____

FINISHED: _____

☆ ☆ ☆ ☆ ☆

FORMAT READ: EBOOK / PRINT / AUDIOBOOK

✓ **SYNOPSIS/THINGS I LIKED:**

_____
_____
_____
_____
_____

🚫 **THINGS I DIDN'T LIKE:**

_____
_____
_____
_____
_____

📝 **FAVORITE QUOTE(S):**

_____
_____
_____
_____
_____
_____
_____
_____

TITLE: _____

GENRE: _____

SERIES: _____

AUTHOR: _____

PAGES: _____

STARTED: _____

FINISHED: _____

☆ ☆ ☆ ☆ ☆

FORMAT READ: EBOOK / PRINT / AUDIOBOOK

✔ **SYNOPSIS/THINGS I LIKED:**

_____
_____
_____
_____

🚫 **THINGS I DIDN'T LIKE:**

_____
_____
_____
_____

✏️ **FAVORITE QUOTE(S):**

_____
_____
_____
_____
_____
_____
_____

☑ **SYNOPSIS/THINGS I LIKED:**

_____
_____
_____
_____

🚫 **THINGS I DIDN'T LIKE:**

_____
_____
_____
_____

✏️ **FAVORITE QUOTE(S):**

_____
_____
_____
_____
_____
_____
_____

TITLE: _____

GENRE: _____

SERIES: _____

AUTHOR: _____

PAGES: _____

STARTED: _____

FINISHED: _____

☆ ☆ ☆ ☆ ☆

FORMAT READ: EBOOK / PRINT / AUDIOBOOK

211

✓ **Synopsis/Things I liked:**

_____

_____

_____

_____

🚫 **Things I didn't like:**

_____

_____

_____

_____

✏️ **Favorite quote(s):**

_____

_____

_____

_____

_____

_____

Title: _____

Genre: _____

Series: _____

Author: _____

Pages: _____

Started: _____

Finished: _____

☆☆☆☆☆

Format read: Ebook / Print / Audiobook

TITLE: _____

GENRE: _____

SERIES: _____

AUTHOR: _____

PAGES: _____

STARTED: _____

FINISHED: _____

☆☆☆☆☆

FORMAT READ: EBOOK / PRINT / AUDIOBOOK

✓ **SYNOPSIS/THINGS I LIKED:**

_____

_____

_____

_____

🚫 **THINGS I DIDN'T LIKE:**

_____

_____

_____

_____

✎ **FAVORITE QUOTE(S):**

_____

_____

_____

_____

_____

_____

_____

213

TITLE: _____

GENRE: _____

SERIES: _____

AUTHOR: _____

PAGES: _____

STARTED: _____

FINISHED: _____

☆☆☆☆☆

FORMAT READ: EBOOK / PRINT / AUDIOBOOK

✓ **SYNOPSIS/THINGS I LIKED:**

_____
_____
_____
_____
_____

🚫 **THINGS I DIDN'T LIKE:**

_____
_____
_____
_____

✎ **FAVORITE QUOTE(S):**

_____
_____
_____
_____
_____
_____
_____

☑ **SYNOPSIS/THINGS I LIKED:**

_____
_____
_____
_____
_____

🚫 **THINGS I DIDN'T LIKE:**

_____
_____
_____
_____

📝 **FAVORITE QUOTE(S):**

_____
_____
_____
_____
_____
_____
_____

TITLE: _____

GENRE: _____

SERIES: _____

AUTHOR: _____

PAGES: _____

STARTED: _____

FINISHED: _____

☆☆☆☆☆

FORMAT READ: EBOOK / PRINT / AUDIOBOOK

✓ **SYNOPSIS/THINGS I LIKED:**

_____

_____

_____

_____

_____

🚫 **THINGS I DIDN'T LIKE:**

_____

_____

_____

_____

✎ **FAVORITE QUOTE(S):**

_____

_____

_____

_____

_____

_____

TITLE: _____

GENRE: _____

SERIES: _____

AUTHOR: _____

PAGES: _____

STARTED: _____

FINISHED: _____

☆ ☆ ☆ ☆ ☆

FORMAT READ: EBOOK / PRINT / AUDIOBOOK

216

TITLE: _____

GENRE: _____

SERIES: _____

AUTHOR: _____

PAGES: _____

STARTED: _____

FINISHED: _____

☆☆☆☆☆

FORMAT READ: EBOOK / PRINT / AUDIOBOOK

✓ SYNOPSIS/THINGS I LIKED:

_____
_____
_____
_____

🚫 THINGS I DIDN'T LIKE:

_____
_____
_____
_____

✏️ FAVORITE QUOTE(S):

_____
_____
_____
_____
_____
_____
_____

TITLE: _____

GENRE: _____

SERIES: _____

AUTHOR: _____

PAGES: _____

STARTED: _____

FINISHED: _____

☆ ☆ ☆ ☆ ☆

FORMAT READ: EBOOK / PRINT / AUDIOBOOK

✔ **SYNOPSIS/THINGS I LIKED:**

_____
_____
_____
_____

🚫 **THINGS I DIDN'T LIKE:**

_____
_____
_____
_____

✎ **FAVORITE QUOTE(S):**

_____
_____
_____
_____
_____
_____

✓ SYNOPSIS/THINGS I LIKED:

_____
_____
_____
_____
_____

🚫 THINGS I DIDN'T LIKE:

_____
_____
_____
_____

✎ FAVORITE QUOTE(S):

_____
_____
_____
_____
_____
_____

TITLE: _____

GENRE: _____

SERIES: _____

AUTHOR: _____

PAGES: _____

STARTED: _____

FINISHED: _____

☆ ☆ ☆ ☆ ☆

FORMAT READ: EBOOK / PRINT / AUDIOBOOK

✅ **SYNOPSIS/THINGS I LIKED:**

_____

_____

_____

_____

_____

🚫 **THINGS I DIDN'T LIKE:**

_____

_____

_____

_____

📝 **FAVORITE QUOTE(S):**

_____

_____

_____

_____

_____

_____

TITLE: _____

GENRE: _____

SERIES: _____

AUTHOR: _____

PAGES: _____

STARTED: _____

FINISHED: _____

☆ ☆ ☆ ☆ ☆

FORMAT READ: EBOOK / PRINT / AUDIOBOOK

TITLE: _____

GENRE: _____

SERIES: _____

AUTHOR: _____

PAGES: _____

STARTED: _____

FINISHED: _____

☆☆☆☆☆

FORMAT READ: EBOOK / PRINT / AUDIOBOOK

✔ SYNOPSIS/THINGS I LIKED:

_____
_____
_____
_____
_____

🚫 THINGS I DIDN'T LIKE:

_____
_____
_____
_____

✏ FAVORITE QUOTE(S):

_____
_____
_____
_____
_____
_____
_____

TITLE: _____

GENRE: _____

SERIES: _____

AUTHOR: _____

PAGES: _____

STARTED: _____

FINISHED: _____

☆ ☆ ☆ ☆ ☆

FORMAT READ: EBOOK / PRINT / AUDIOBOOK

✔ **SYNOPSIS/THINGS I LIKED:**

_____
_____
_____
_____

🚫 **THINGS I DIDN'T LIKE:**

_____
_____
_____
_____

✎ **FAVORITE QUOTE(S):**

_____
_____
_____
_____
_____
_____
_____

_____

_____

_____

_____

_____

🚫 **THINGS I DIDN'T LIKE:**

_____

_____

_____

_____

✎ **FAVORITE QUOTE(S):**

_____

_____

_____

_____

_____

_____

TITLE: _____

GENRE: _____

SERIES: _____

AUTHOR: _____

PAGES: _____

STARTED: _____

FINISHED: _____

☆ ☆ ☆ ☆ ☆

FORMAT READ: EBOOK / PRINT / AUDIOBOOK

223

☑ SYNOPSIS/THINGS I LIKED:

_____

_____

_____

_____

_____

🚫 THINGS I DIDN'T LIKE:

_____

_____

_____

_____

🖊 FAVORITE QUOTE(S):

_____

_____

_____

_____

_____

_____

TITLE: _____

GENRE: _____

SERIES: _____

AUTHOR: _____

PAGES: _____

STARTED: _____

FINISHED: _____

☆ ☆ ☆ ☆ ☆

FORMAT READ: EBOOK / PRINT / AUDIOBOOK

TITLE: _____

GENRE: _____

SERIES: _____

AUTHOR: _____

PAGES: _____

STARTED: _____

FINISHED: _____

☆ ☆ ☆ ☆ ☆

FORMAT READ: EBOOK / PRINT / AUDIOBOOK

✓ SYNOPSIS/THINGS I LIKED:

_____
_____
_____
_____

🚫 THINGS I DIDN'T LIKE:

_____
_____
_____
_____

✎ FAVORITE QUOTE(S):

_____
_____
_____
_____
_____
_____
_____
_____

TITLE: _____

GENRE: _____

SERIES: _____

AUTHOR: _____

PAGES: _____

STARTED: _____

FINISHED: _____

☆☆☆☆☆

FORMAT READ: EBOOK / PRINT / AUDIOBOOK

✅ **SYNOPSIS/THINGS I LIKED:**

_____
_____
_____
_____

🚫 **THINGS I DIDN'T LIKE:**

_____
_____
_____
_____

📝 **FAVORITE QUOTE(S):**

_____
_____
_____
_____
_____
_____
_____

✓ **SYNOPSIS/THINGS I LIKED:**

_____

_____

_____

_____

🚫 **THINGS I DIDN'T LIKE:**

_____

_____

_____

_____

✏️ **FAVORITE QUOTE(S):**

_____

_____

_____

_____

_____

_____

TITLE: _____

GENRE: _____

SERIES: _____

AUTHOR: _____

PAGES: _____

STARTED: _____

FINISHED: _____

☆ ☆ ☆ ☆ ☆

FORMAT READ: EBOOK / PRINT / AUDIOBOOK

✓ **SYNOPSIS/THINGS I LIKED:**

_____

_____

_____

_____

🚫 **THINGS I DIDN'T LIKE:**

_____

_____

_____

_____

✏️ **FAVORITE QUOTE(S):**

_____

_____

_____

_____

_____

_____

TITLE: _____

GENRE: _____

SERIES: _____

AUTHOR: _____

PAGES: _____

STARTED: _____

FINISHED: _____

☆ ☆ ☆ ☆ ☆

FORMAT READ: EBOOK / PRINT / AUDIOBOOK

TITLE: _____

GENRE: _____

SERIES: _____

AUTHOR: _____

PAGES: _____

STARTED: _____

FINISHED: _____

☆☆☆☆☆

FORMAT READ: EBOOK / PRINT / AUDIOBOOK

✔ **SYNOPSIS/THINGS I LIKED:**

_____
_____
_____
_____

🚫 **THINGS I DIDN'T LIKE:**

_____
_____
_____
_____

✏ **FAVORITE QUOTE(S):**

_____
_____
_____
_____
_____
_____
_____

TITLE: _____

GENRE: _____

SERIES: _____

AUTHOR: _____

PAGES: _____

STARTED: _____

FINISHED: _____

☆ ☆ ☆ ☆ ☆

FORMAT READ: EBOOK / PRINT / AUDIOBOOK

✓ **SYNOPSIS/THINGS I LIKED:**

_____
_____
_____
_____

🚫 **THINGS I DIDN'T LIKE:**

_____
_____
_____
_____

✎ **FAVORITE QUOTE(S):**

_____
_____
_____
_____
_____
_____
_____

✓ **Synopsis/Things I liked:**

_____

_____

_____

_____

🚫 **Things I didn't like:**

_____

_____

_____

_____

🖊 **Favorite quote(s):**

_____

_____

_____

_____

_____

_____

_____

Title: _____

Genre: _____

Series: _____

Author: _____

Pages: _____

Started: _____

Finished: _____

☆ ☆ ☆ ☆ ☆

Format read: Ebook / Print / Audiobook

✅ SYNOPSIS/THINGS I LIKED:

_____
_____
_____
_____
_____

🚫 THINGS I DIDN'T LIKE:

_____
_____
_____
_____
_____

📝 FAVORITE QUOTE(S):

_____
_____
_____
_____
_____
_____
_____

TITLE: _____

GENRE: _____

SERIES: _____

AUTHOR: _____

PAGES: _____

STARTED: _____

FINISHED: _____

☆ ☆ ☆ ☆ ☆

FORMAT READ: EBOOK / PRINT / AUDIOBOOK

Title: _____

Genre: _____

Series: _____

Author: _____

Pages: _____

Started: _____

Finished: _____

☆ ☆ ☆ ☆ ☆

FORMAT READ: EBOOK / PRINT / AUDIOBOOK

✓ **Synopsis/Things I liked:**

_____
_____
_____
_____

🚫 **Things I didn't like:**

_____
_____
_____
_____

✎ **Favorite quote(s):**

_____
_____
_____
_____
_____
_____

TITLE: _____

GENRE: _____

SERIES: _____

AUTHOR: _____

PAGES: _____

STARTED: _____

FINISHED: _____

☆☆☆☆☆

FORMAT READ: EBOOK / PRINT / AUDIOBOOK

✔ **SYNOPSIS/THINGS I LIKED:**

_____
_____
_____
_____

🚫 **THINGS I DIDN'T LIKE:**

_____
_____
_____
_____

📝 **FAVORITE QUOTE(S):**

_____
_____
_____
_____
_____
_____
_____

✓ **SYNOPSIS/THINGS I LIKED:**

_____
_____
_____
_____

🚫 **THINGS I DIDN'T LIKE:**

_____
_____
_____
_____

✎ **FAVORITE QUOTE(S):**

_____
_____
_____
_____
_____
_____
_____

TITLE: _____

GENRE: _____

SERIES: _____

AUTHOR: _____

PAGES: _____

STARTED: _____

FINISHED: _____

☆ ☆ ☆ ☆ ☆

FORMAT READ: EBOOK / PRINT / AUDIOBOOK

✓ **SYNOPSIS/THINGS I LIKED:**

_____

_____

_____

_____

_____

🚫 **THINGS I DIDN'T LIKE:**

_____

_____

_____

_____

_____

✎ **FAVORITE QUOTE(S):**

_____

_____

_____

_____

_____

_____

_____

TITLE: _____

GENRE: _____

SERIES: _____

AUTHOR: _____

PAGES: _____

STARTED: _____

FINISHED: _____

☆ ☆ ☆ ☆ ☆

FORMAT READ: EBOOK / PRINT / AUDIOBOOK

Title: _____

Genre: _____

Series: _____

Author: _____

Pages: _____

Started: _____

Finished: _____

☆ ☆ ☆ ☆ ☆

Format read: Ebook / Print / Audiobook

✓ **Synopsis/Things I liked:**

_____
_____
_____
_____

🚫 **Things I didn't like:**

_____
_____
_____
_____

✎ **Favorite quote(s):**

_____
_____
_____
_____
_____
_____
_____

TITLE: _____

GENRE: _____

SERIES: _____

AUTHOR: _____

PAGES: _____

STARTED: _____

FINISHED: _____

☆☆☆☆☆

FORMAT READ: EBOOK / PRINT / AUDIOBOOK

✓ **SYNOPSIS/THINGS I LIKED:**

_____
_____
_____
_____

🚫 **THINGS I DIDN'T LIKE:**

_____
_____
_____
_____

✎ **FAVORITE QUOTE(S):**

_____
_____
_____
_____
_____
_____
_____

✓ **SYNOPSIS/THINGS I LIKED:**

_____
_____
_____
_____
_____

🚫 **THINGS I DIDN'T LIKE:**

_____
_____
_____
_____

📝 **FAVORITE QUOTE(S):**

_____
_____
_____
_____
_____
_____

TITLE: _____

GENRE: _____

SERIES: _____

AUTHOR: _____

PAGES: _____

STARTED: _____

FINISHED: _____

☆ ☆ ☆ ☆ ☆

FORMAT READ: EBOOK / PRINT / AUDIOBOOK

✓ **SYNOPSIS/THINGS I LIKED:**

_____
_____
_____
_____

🚫 **THINGS I DIDN'T LIKE:**

_____
_____
_____
_____

📝 **FAVORITE QUOTE(S):**

_____
_____
_____
_____
_____
_____
_____

TITLE: _____

GENRE: _____

SERIES: _____

AUTHOR: _____

PAGES: _____

STARTED: _____

FINISHED: _____

☆ ☆ ☆ ☆ ☆

FORMAT READ: EBOOK / PRINT / AUDIOBOOK

TITLE: _____

GENRE: _____

SERIES: _____

AUTHOR: _____

PAGES: _____

STARTED: _____

FINISHED: _____

☆ ☆ ☆ ☆ ☆

FORMAT READ: EBOOK / PRINT / AUDIOBOOK

✓ SYNOPSIS/THINGS I LIKED:

_____
_____
_____
_____

🚫 THINGS I DIDN'T LIKE:

_____
_____
_____
_____

✎ FAVORITE QUOTE(S):

_____
_____
_____
_____
_____
_____
_____

TITLE: _____

GENRE: _____

SERIES: _____

AUTHOR: _____

PAGES: _____

STARTED: _____

FINISHED: _____

☆☆☆☆☆

FORMAT READ: EBOOK / PRINT / AUDIOBOOK

✓ **SYNOPSIS/THINGS I LIKED:**

_____
_____
_____
_____
_____

🚫 **THINGS I DIDN'T LIKE:**

_____
_____
_____
_____
_____

📝 **FAVORITE QUOTE(S):**

_____
_____
_____
_____
_____
_____
_____

✅ SYNOPSIS/THINGS I LIKED:

_____

_____

_____

_____

_____

🚫 THINGS I DIDN'T LIKE:

_____

_____

_____

_____

_____

✒️ FAVORITE QUOTE(S):

_____

_____

_____

_____

_____

_____

_____

TITLE: _____

GENRE: _____

SERIES: _____

AUTHOR: _____

PAGES: _____

STARTED: _____

FINISHED: _____

☆ ☆ ☆ ☆ ☆

FORMAT READ: EBOOK / PRINT / AUDIOBOOK

☑ **SYNOPSIS/THINGS I LIKED:**

_____
_____
_____
_____
_____

🚫 **THINGS I DIDN'T LIKE:**

_____
_____
_____
_____
_____

📝 **FAVORITE QUOTE(S):**

_____
_____
_____
_____
_____
_____
_____

TITLE: _____

GENRE: _____

SERIES: _____

AUTHOR: _____

PAGES: _____

STARTED: _____

FINISHED: _____

☆ ☆ ☆ ☆ ☆

FORMAT READ: EBOOK / PRINT / AUDIOBOOK

TITLE: _____

GENRE: _____

SERIES: _____

AUTHOR: _____

PAGES: _____

STARTED: _____

FINISHED: _____

☆ ☆ ☆ ☆ ☆

FORMAT READ: EBOOK / PRINT / AUDIOBOOK

✓ **SYNOPSIS/THINGS I LIKED:**

_____
_____
_____
_____
_____

🚫 **THINGS I DIDN'T LIKE:**

_____
_____
_____
_____
_____

✎ **FAVORITE QUOTE(S):**

_____
_____
_____
_____
_____
_____
_____

TITLE: _____

GENRE: _____

SERIES: _____

AUTHOR: _____

PAGES: _____

STARTED: _____

FINISHED: _____

☆☆☆☆☆

FORMAT READ: EBOOK / PRINT / AUDIOBOOK

✓ SYNOPSIS/THINGS I LIKED:

_____
_____
_____
_____
_____

🚫 THINGS I DIDN'T LIKE:

_____
_____
_____
_____
_____

✏️ FAVORITE QUOTE(S):

_____
_____
_____
_____
_____
_____
_____

✔ **SYNOPSIS/THINGS I LIKED:**

_____
_____
_____
_____

🚫 **THINGS I DIDN'T LIKE:**

_____
_____
_____
_____

📝 **FAVORITE QUOTE(S):**

_____
_____
_____
_____
_____
_____

TITLE: _____

GENRE: _____

SERIES: _____

AUTHOR: _____

PAGES: _____

STARTED: _____

FINISHED: _____

☆ ☆ ☆ ☆ ☆

FORMAT READ: EBOOK / PRINT / AUDIOBOOK

✔ **SYNOPSIS/THINGS I LIKED:**

_____
_____
_____
_____

🚫 **THINGS I DIDN'T LIKE:**

_____
_____
_____
_____

✎ **FAVORITE QUOTE(S):**

_____
_____
_____
_____
_____
_____

TITLE: _____

GENRE: _____

SERIES: _____

AUTHOR: _____

PAGES: _____

STARTED: _____

FINISHED: _____

☆ ☆ ☆ ☆ ☆

FORMAT READ: EBOOK / PRINT / AUDIOBOOK

TITLE: _____

GENRE: _____

SERIES: _____

AUTHOR: _____

PAGES: _____

STARTED: _____

FINISHED: _____

☆ ☆ ☆ ☆ ☆

FORMAT READ: EBOOK / PRINT / AUDIOBOOK

✓ **SYNOPSIS/THINGS I LIKED:**

_____
_____
_____
_____

🚫 **THINGS I DIDN'T LIKE:**

_____
_____
_____
_____

✎ **FAVORITE QUOTE(S):**

_____
_____
_____
_____
_____
_____
_____

TITLE: _____

GENRE: _____

SERIES: _____

AUTHOR: _____

PAGES: _____

STARTED: _____

FINISHED: _____

☆☆☆☆☆

FORMAT READ: EBOOK / PRINT / AUDIOBOOK

✓ **SYNOPSIS/THINGS I LIKED:**

_____
_____
_____
_____

🚫 **THINGS I DIDN'T LIKE:**

_____
_____
_____
_____

✏️ **FAVORITE QUOTE(S):**

_____
_____
_____
_____
_____
_____
_____

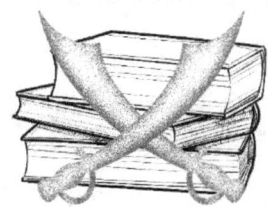

THE DUSTY
DNFs
(DID NOT FINISH)

TITLE/PROGRESS:

COMMENTARY:

TITLE/PROGRESS:

COMMENTARY:

TITLE/PROGRESS:

COMMENTARY:

TITLE/PROGRESS:

COMMENTARY:

TITLE/PROGRESS:

COMMENTARY:

TITLE/PROGRESS:

COMMENTARY:

TITLE/PROGRESS:

COMMENTARY:

TITLE/PROGRESS:

COMMENTARY:

TITLE/PROGRESS:

COMMENTARY:

TITLE/PROGRESS:

COMMENTARY:

TITLE/PROGRESS:

COMMENTARY:

TITLE/PROGRESS:

COMMENTARY:

The Dusty
DNFs
(Did Not Finish)

Title/Progress:

Commentary:

Title/Progress:

Commentary:

Title/Progress:

Commentary:

Title/Progress:

Commentary:

Title/Progress:

Commentary:

Title/Progress:

Commentary:

Title/Progress:

Commentary:

Title/Progress:

Commentary:

Title/Progress:

Commentary:

Title/Progress:

Commentary:

Title/Progress:

Commentary:

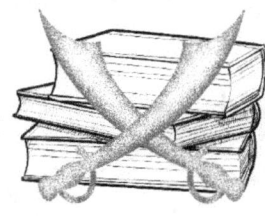

THE DUSTY
DNFs
(DID NOT FINISH)

TITLE/PROGRESS:
_____

COMMENTARY:
_____

TITLE/PROGRESS:
_____

COMMENTARY:
_____

TITLE/PROGRESS:
_____

COMMENTARY:
_____

TITLE/PROGRESS:
_____

COMMENTARY:
_____

TITLE/PROGRESS:
_____

COMMENTARY:
_____

TITLE/PROGRESS:
_____

COMMENTARY:
_____

TITLE/PROGRESS:
_____

COMMENTARY:
_____

TITLE/PROGRESS:
_____

COMMENTARY:
_____

TITLE/PROGRESS:
_____

COMMENTARY:
_____

TITLE/PROGRESS:
_____

COMMENTARY:
_____

TITLE/PROGRESS:
_____

COMMENTARY:
_____

TITLE/PROGRESS:
_____

COMMENTARY:

THE DUSTY
DNFs
(DID NOT FINISH)

TITLE/PROGRESS:
_____

COMMENTARY:
_____

TITLE/PROGRESS:
_____

COMMENTARY:
_____

TITLE/PROGRESS:
_____

COMMENTARY:
_____

TITLE/PROGRESS:
_____

COMMENTARY:
_____

TITLE/PROGRESS:
_____

COMMENTARY:
_____

TITLE/PROGRESS:
_____

COMMENTARY:
_____

TITLE/PROGRESS:
_____

COMMENTARY:
_____

TITLE/PROGRESS:
_____

COMMENTARY:
_____

TITLE/PROGRESS:
_____

COMMENTARY:
_____

TITLE/PROGRESS:
_____

COMMENTARY:
_____

TITLE/PROGRESS:
_____

COMMENTARY:
_____

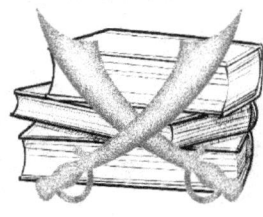

THE DUSTY
DNFS
(DID NOT FINISH)

TITLE/PROGRESS:

COMMENTARY:

TITLE/PROGRESS:

COMMENTARY:

TITLE/PROGRESS:

COMMENTARY:

TITLE/PROGRESS:

COMMENTARY:

TITLE/PROGRESS:

COMMENTARY:

TITLE/PROGRESS:

COMMENTARY:

TITLE/PROGRESS:

COMMENTARY:

TITLE/PROGRESS:

COMMENTARY:

TITLE/PROGRESS:

COMMENTARY:

TITLE/PROGRESS:

COMMENTARY:

TITLE/PROGRESS:

COMMENTARY:

TITLE/PROGRESS:

COMMENTARY:

THE DUSTY
DNFs
(DID NOT FINISH)

TITLE/PROGRESS:

COMMENTARY:

TITLE/PROGRESS:

COMMENTARY:

TITLE/PROGRESS:

COMMENTARY:

TITLE/PROGRESS:

COMMENTARY:

TITLE/PROGRESS:

COMMENTARY:

TITLE/PROGRESS:

COMMENTARY:

TITLE/PROGRESS:

COMMENTARY:

TITLE/PROGRESS:

COMMENTARY:

TITLE/PROGRESS:

COMMENTARY:

TITLE/PROGRESS:

COMMENTARY:

TITLE/PROGRESS:

COMMENTARY:

TITLE/PROGRESS:

COMMENTARY:

Grab your replacement book journal!

Pick up your next volume now!

Paper and Ink Trophies and *Gems & Genres* are both premium book journals also offered by Painted Wings Publishing. They each accommodate entries for 250 books and have individual aesthetic touches.

For more information, go to JHouserWrites.com

Book Recommendations

THE SEEDER WARS TRILOGY   THE HEIR'S DUOLOGY

Seeder Wars is a Young Adult Contemporary Romantic Fantasy series featuring unique magic, botanical beings, spies, & assassins. The series starts with a central trilogy and expands to a spin-off duology (& more on the way!)

Magic in the Match
Fairy Tale
Romances

Magic in the Match is a series of standalone Adult Fairy Tale Sweet Romances.

The Hatanii Bride is a novelette inspired by a Polish fairy tale (*The Unlooked-for Prince*), set in a Polynesian atmosphere, and has all the best tropes—arranged marriage, enemies-to-lovers, and more!

The Dream Trials is a novelette retelling of a Dutch fairy tale (*The Princess and the Pea*). After being caught in an enchanted rainfall following the queen's passing, Maribel's nights are plagued with strange dreams, her days full of pain and mystery—all preparing her for something she never could have imagined.

More information on JHouserWrites.com!

www.ingramcontent.com/pod-product-compliance
Lightning Source LLC
Chambersburg PA
CBHW061129120626
46546CB00005B/1719